THE
Compliment
Quotient

Praise for *The Compliment Quotient*

"*The Compliment Quotient* has turned me on to the Power of Compliments and enhanced my relationships, my parenting and even my business success. I've tried the methods in this gem of a book and they have turned around many a sticky (or stinky) situation-- from a grumpy mood (mine) to a marital squabble. Monica Strobel's "complimentology" techniques transform turbulence and tempers into triumph and ta-da. More important, implemented regularly, you can avoid much stress and unhappiness by being proactive with these simple and powerful ideas and tools."

> — Lisa Tener, writing coach and author, *The Ultimate Guide to Transforming Anger*, www.lisatener.com, *Bring Your Book to Life*

"As an expert in the art of conversation, I know that giving compliments is a wonderful way to break the ice in social situations. *The Compliment Quotient* helps you understand this and the many other benefits of adopting a habit of giving more compliments to those around you. I coach my readers to make conversation with at least three new people a week and as author Monica Strobel outlines, using compliments is an excellent way to get their attention."

> — Debra Fine, bestselling author of *The Fine Art of Small Talk: How to Start a Conversation, Keep it Going, Build Networking Skills-- and Leave a Positive Impression*

"I frequently speak about how simple, kind actions can transform your life and relationships. In *The Compliment Quotient*, author Monica Strobel outlines quick, practical ways to add more positive words of praise to uplift your own spirits while spreading the vibrations of love, gratitude and acceptance to others."

> — Mary Morrissey, bestselling author of *No Less Than Greatness and Building Your Field of Dreams*, president and founder of LifeSOULutions

Praise for *The Compliment Quotient*

"*The Compliment Quotient* offers a simple, compelling strategy for putting more zest and great feelings into busy days. Monica Strobel reminds us that we may not always have time for a yoga pose or meditation, but there's an easy way to reduce stress and boost the quality of our lives--and those around us. It's a joy to offer my compliments to Monica Strobel!"
> – Tama J. Kieves, bestselling author of *THIS TIME I DANCE! Creating the Work You Love* and Founder and President of Awakening Artistry. (AwakeningArtistry.com)

"Taking action is key to getting off the self-help treadmill, and as Monica Strobel outlines in *The Compliment Quotient*, is one of the ways compliments are more powerful than we think. In her book, she reveals how taking the opportunity to make a difference by giving someone a compliment means a huge difference in your own attitude and success."
> – Kristen Moeller bestselling author of *Waiting for Jack Confessions of a Self-Help Junkie* and author coach: *Author YOUR Brilliance™ Programs*

"As someone who is a certified Energy Leadership™ Master Practitioner, I knew right away that Monica Strobel was onto something with *The Compliment Quotient*. In the 7 levels of energy in this approach, a compliment can move you up 3-5 levels in an instant. So every time you choose to freely give a compliment, you are choosing a new future for yourself. It takes courage to compliment, but how excitingly simple is that?"
> – Darla LeDoux CPC, ACC, ELI-MP, *Living Your Sweet Spot Coach and Guide*

"*The Compliment Quotient* is brimming with ideas about how women can use praise and kind words to keep their joy and energy flowing. One of the Inspirational Coffee Club's Ground Rules for Savoring Life is to "take time to fill another's cup," and author Monica Strobel's strategies for giving compliments to family, friends and others provide easy-to-follow ways to keep your own spirits simmering while you share your loving inspiration with others."
> – Julie Clark, founder of *The Inspirational Coffee Club* and best-selling author of *Inspirational Coffee Breaks for Women* (www.theinspirationalcoffeeclub.com)

THE
Compliment
Quotient

Boost Your Spirits,
Spark Your Relationships,
and Uplift the World

*Adam —
You are brilliant!
— Monica*

Monica Strobel

The Compliment Quotient: Boost Your Spirits,
Spark Your Relationships and Uplift the World

by Monica Strobel

ISBN 978-1-936214-37-2

Library of Congress Control Number: 2010943048

Published by Wise Roads Press, An Imprint of Wyatt-MacKenzie

For speaking appearances, interviews or other bookings, please
contact Monica Strobel at monicastrobel@gmail.com
or visit www.complimentquotient.com
Wise Roads LLC PO Box 3615 Littleton, CO 80122

Quantity orders and promotional partnerships available.
Book interior design by www.DesignZoneUSA.com

Wise**Roads**
PRESS

an Imprint of

Wyatt-MacKenzie Publishing
DEADWOOD, OREGON
www.wyattmackenzie.com

DEDICATION

*For **Mom** and **Dad**,*
for their practical wisdom
and unending love.

*For **Amy**, with whose generous,*
loving friendship I was blessed,
which buoyed me along life's
journey and whose caring
presence will always be
a part of us.

CONTENTS

SECTION FOUR
The Compliment Quotient Way of Life

INTRODUCTION

Attitude, Relationships and Love

ould your relationships use a pick-me-up? Are you looking for more zest in your day-to-day doings? Would you like to experience deeper, more succulent connections with those around you?

For years I have heard that the road to living more joyfully and being happy in my relationships and circumstances comes by driving through life with the right attitude—a positive attitude, a grateful, see-and-savor-the-small-things attitude. One of my favorite motivational speakers, Earl Nightingale, dubbed attitude "the magic word," and stated that the right attitude was a key element for any success in life, including in our relationships. Similarly, American philosopher William James stated, "[T]here is one factor that can make the difference between damaging your relationship and deepening it. That factor is attitude."

As someone who looks at life through an optimistic lens, I've seen how this power of positive attitude works. Yet the problem is, how do you keep your spirits up, your joy flowing, and your relationships humming along on a daily and sometimes moment-to-moment basis amidst this thing called living our lives? Especially when:

> You're up to your elbows in diapers and dirty
> dishes, book reports and soccer games.

All you seem to focus on is what everyone else has and what you can't afford.

You're so deep into routine and responsibility that you can hardly remember the spark that drew you and your partner together in the first place.

Like other busy women, I've faced these challenges and more as I've juggled the responsibilities of a working person, wife, mother, friend, sister, school volunteer, homemaker, chauffeur, and committee member. In the midst of joy-killing, relationship-quashing situations, I couldn't drop into a yoga pose, pull out my notebook to review my positive affirmations, or do a deep-breathing visualization. Instead, I learned to use a simple yet powerful force to alter my state of being at any time. I began to harness the power of giving compliments – to achieve a more uplifted, accepting and peaceful personal attitude, as well as positively influence those around me.

But using compliments as a life-enhancing tool? You may wonder about this. After all, you may think compliments are merely part of manners or etiquette. Or you may feel that compliments should be reserved for something big—only exchanged when really earned by some outstanding action. But I think most of us have underestimated the power in this one simple practice. In reality, the small, seemingly lightweight compliment is a potent force that has the ability to transform our relationships—and when our relationships are working, we are more likely to find day-to-day joy and fulfillment. A simple compliment has the power to lift our spirits at virtually any time we choose. In addition, a compliment practice contributes to the uplifting of the positive energy all around us.

Having grown up in a large, Midwestern family, I learned early the importance of acting respectful and being kind to others—though often more through deeds than spoken words. After decades on life's highways and byways, my "take care of others" outlook grew into a habit of complimenting those close to me, which then developed into a practice of sprinkling compliments among more casual acquaintances and total strangers, too. I found I could easily boost my joy by offering words of praise, even in the types of challenging situations in which you may find yourself as well, such as:

> Getting caught up in arguments with my spouse about the same little things over and over again;

> Crossing a gulf that arose in a friendship that's been diluted from lack of time and attention;

> Struggling to bring more romance and lightness back into my relationship;

> Finding that I have been spending too much time complaining and not enough time being the loving presence I want to be in the world.

The Compliment Quotient is a guide to helping you unleash the power of compliments in your life and relationships. It is designed to stimulate a profound re-alignment of your heart-energy, to experience an unfolding of love and your deeper sense of expressing it. This book is for anyone who wants to cultivate more love and less separation. This book is for anyone who wants to create more success and less conflict. This book is for anyone who wants to contribute to a more constructive world and lessen the discord around us.

By increasing your understanding of this compelling force, you can embark upon your own journey to forge new and vigorous connections with your loved ones and brighten up dull or monotonous day-to-day moments— by fine-tuning your awareness of those around you and expressing yourself in lively, meaningful and heart-felt compliments.

In detailing the power of offering simple, kind words to others, this book will cover, among other things: why compliments are more powerful than you may have realized; what makes an effective compliment; and strategies for using compliments in five of our most important relationships.

You'll also find specific, hands-on exercises and suggestions that work for both jumping into the regular practice of complimenting and expanding the reach of your comments. You can use these lessons, designed for busy, doing-it-all people, to fertilize relationships that are most compelling or most troublesome, or just to sprinkle joy throughout your interactions and your life.

Implementing this approach won't take tons of time or require you to get an advanced degree or hire a trainer, therapist or coach —though there's nothing wrong with any of those! All you have to do is weave a compliment habit into your daily doings. That said, reaping the rewards of new behavior does take a little practice. Like anything, it grows into itself the more you embrace it. So don't just read this book and consider your task finished. Whether you start gradually, by using more compliments in one relationship or offering a few compliments in several relationships, or by adopting a full-on compliment practice, you'll need to take these lessons out into your everyday life.

I'm excited to share why you should raise your compliment quotient and how to do it. Join me to reap profound, life-affirming benefits as you amplify your understanding and use of this compelling force.

SECTION ONE

UNLOCKING YOUR COMPLIMENT QUOTIENT

CHAPTER ONE

Why Compliments, Why Now?

*We cannot hold a torch to
light another's path without
brightening our own.*

~Ben Sweetland

*Man is a knot into which
relationships are tied.*

~Antoine de Saint-Exupéry,
Flight to Arras

hat do you romanticize about? My nighttime fantasies stream less along the lines of leaping through waves on the beach or wearing glass slippers to a ball, and more in line with having undone work magically finished overnight, á la *The Shoemaker and The Elves*. Remember that tale? The shoemaker leaves his last leather on his cobbler's bench when he goes to sleep and awakes to find a beautifully crafted, finished pair of footwear in its place—the work of helpful elves, as it turns out.

Instead, I awake to the laundry wrinkled in the dryer, the dishwasher not run and emails overflowing my inbox, visited not by the helpful and talented elves of shoemaking fame, but by the mischievous ones from the Murphy's Law family tree who happily disrupt already full-to-the-brim mornings. Not long ago, for example, I had to get to a coffee shop near my office for a morning meeting that had taken a few weeks to schedule—an important link to upcoming work. My youngest had forgotten to mention until saying goodnight the evening before that she had a Student Council commitment the next morning. That meant we would need to be out the door 15 minutes earlier than normal, which wouldn't be easy.

The meeting called for a more professional look than my usual routine, which led to that harried morning "what to wear" search. After quickly rejecting two outfits—one just not right and one just not fitting right—

I started putting things on that I knew fit but hadn't worn together before: a bright dress, a short-sleeved cardigan and a trusty (read: *old*) standby necklace I usually saved for going out. Finally, I headed downstairs, only to remember that I had washed my son's jeans the night before but had forgotten to dry them. I threw them into the dryer—pulling them out only 20 minutes later, so he wore them with damp, cold pockets and waistband. Then, breakfast rushed through, lunches made, tea kettle off, cats fed, lights out, work bag, backpacks and books all gathered, we made it out the door barely in the nick of time.

After skating into the coffee shop a miraculous few minutes early, I gazed at the folks scattered around, studying faces, since I didn't know what two of the people I was meeting looked like. When no one returned my quizzical glances, I placed my order with the barrista behind the counter. She responded morning-efficient friendly and, after working her magic on the coffee contraption, was about to hand over my cup when she said, "I was going to tell you how pretty your necklace was." Then she paused.

My hand dropped, and I looked back at her, thinking, "That's odd. Tell someone you were going to say something nice, but decide not to? Decide to take it back? Maybe I didn't get my outfit right, or my hair's messed up or...." She interrupted my rising tide of downbeat self-talk to finish her statement. "I was going to tell you how pretty your necklace was. But after you ordered and stepped back, I saw your dress, and I decided to tell you your whole outfit looks pretty." She wasn't overly effervescent—after all, it was still early—but her words caught me pleasantly off guard.

"Thanks so much. I really appreciate hearing it," I said, grinning as I turned around, feeling not on top of the world but jolted out of the morning's earlier anxiety. I won't claim I experienced leap-over-tall-buildings inner power, but I did feel an immediate change of inner-atmosphere that let me shake off the morning's upset rhythm and follow a positive melody moving forward into my meeting. I even had a few more smiles later, remembering her comment, which continued to add some sunshine to the rest of my day.

This illustrates how simple yet life altering a shared positive acknowledgment can be. As Benjamin Franklin wrote, "Human felicity is produced not as much by great pieces of good fortune that seldom happen as by little advantages that occur every day."

Do you remember a compliment that affected you or your day? Have you found yourself smiling hours after getting a quick acknowledgement from your spouse—or even a stranger? Have you considered how the nature of your relationship would change if you quit criticizing your partner or your child and focused on what they were doing right? Do you ever consider what anxiety you might quell or misgiving you might calm—or joy *you* would reap—with a heartfelt, admiring comment?

You may, as I do, generally feel that you're living the good life, a life rich with activity and fulfillment. You're settling into marriage or a committed relationship. You're busily raising your kids. You're moving along in your career, roosting in a neighborhood and keeping in touch with friends and family. And yet, even without gaping holes in your daily satisfaction, if you're like most of us, you find smaller gaps, little moth-eaten places in your life and relationships that diminish your attitude, focus and feelings of connection and purpose, yet you don't have the time or energy to stop and mend the holes.

Even if we feel we are on the right track in our lives, appreciating our essential abundance and recognizing our happiness, we can experience situations that nip at our heels and grow through stress, hurriedness, or apathy into more dangerous predators of our satisfaction and joy.

Yet women are supposed to excel at relationships, right? After all, we've been told that we garner success not by competing with others, but by seeking compromise and camaraderie. Our relationships serve not just as the framework of our lives; we often measure our personal value and satisfaction by the quality of our relationships. But while we seek fulfillment through personal connections, they can also be the source of troublesome challenges.

In our romantic relationships, for example, once we've left the easy and endearing stage behind, we often find we have to work harder to feel that closeness and attachment to our mates. We aggravate each other with little missteps and outright disagreements, which create cracks that take more time and energy to fill in and smooth over.

At home with our children, we hope for more meaningful interactions but too often go into autopilot. We focus on homework, shuttling kids to activities and reminding them about what they forgot to do – not just once, but annoyingly over and over.

At the office, we're thrown in with coworkers who have been chosen more for their skill sets than whether or not they get along with others well during the long hours at work. We deal with offensive habits, difficult personalities and even office rage.

And when it comes to our girlfriends, we get together less often and let someone else offer the support we used to give naturally and regularly. Or maybe we've moved to be closer to a job and find ourselves thrown into new surroundings, forced to build relationships in a world where everyone's cups are full and their friendships already overflowing.

On top of this hodge-podge of internalized tension, we live in a popular culture that seems to be growing ever more fractured and unfeeling. Daily, we're confronted with the impersonal where we used to have connections. We're faced with figuring out automated phone menus; merging into a line of indifferent motorists on a crowded highway; listening to foul-mouthed rants behind us at baseball games—all contributing to our sense of an expanding "culture of callousness."

While we may believe that small annoyances are just that–small—recent studies suggest otherwise. Findings indicate that the sum of these lesser hassles may actually equal more stress than a major incident. Like that pebble in our shoe that we don't bother stopping to take out, these seemingly little frustrations eventually exact a toll on our attitudes and emotions. Scientists have confirmed that these outwardly small these frustrations, such as your spouse putting off cleaning the gutters or your sister going shopping for mom's present without you—even the juice stain you ignore on the carpet— build up from one day to the next. Over the long term, they set the stage for cancers and other physical and mental health problems.

So, what if we slowed our frantic pace and took the time to focus in on what's working rather than what's not working? What if we took time to notice the things about others that make them stand out, that they do with little effort—the things that we usually take for granted or overlook—and shared those through a consistent practice of complimenting? What if we didn't pass up ordinary opportunities to say something nice because they don't seem like big enough reasons, or even because we're worried what others will think of what we're saying? How much better would we weather all those small irritations and bridge the cracks in our relationships?

Just as it's the little things that end up turning those fissures in our lives into huge chasms, so too can the small things we do add up to significant moments we most cherish. Over the years, I have undertaken a seemingly small but distinct effort to regularly acknowledge those around me, dedicating time and energy to look for something special to highlight about them. I've complimented a friend when she was asked to participate on a new committee at work. I've complimented my son when he turned in his homework on time. I've complimented colleagues when they got a project off to a good start. I've complimented my husband on being a great kisser. I've complimented strangers on wearing a color that looks particularly good on them. I've complimented my daughter on being a good friend. These are just a few of the thousands more expressions of praise and admiration I've shared with those around me.

Offering these appreciative, admiring thoughts have given me some of the most instantaneously gratifying experiences I have ever had. Interacting with others in this way has been nothing short of transformative—and not just in my relationships with others. It has had a surprisingly fortifying effect on me, too.

We instinctively understand the effect a compliment has on the *receiver*. For instance, my daughter recently recalled to me the exact day and place nearly a year ago that someone told her she was beautiful, a comment that helped buoy her tenuous, young-teen self-image. But through my practice of dedicated complimenting, I have also unearthed the tangible benefit complimenting has on the *giver*. We enjoy the juiciness of life by taking a bigger bite, and freely giving compliments is part of how we get to the moist, luscious center.

The practice of complimenting is one of the most effective ways to boost our own joyful feelings, spur a heartfelt bond with loved ones or friends, and combat the sometimes-enormous feelings of stress, detachment, distance, or loneliness we all experience from time to time. The graciousness and generosity embodied in any one genuine compliment is another strand of connection and meaning in our relationships with those important to us.

At this time of complexity and busy-ness, many of us have already started to look for ways to clear out the clutter and find a simpler way of living. The beauty of the common compliment is exactly that – a simple tool completely accessible to all of us regardless of age, experience, education, spiritual practice or other beliefs. It's easy to embrace, appeals to our inherent good sense, and, maybe most importantly, is in sync with the intuitive, heart-centered approach to life at which women excel.

The act of giving compliments draws on the wellspring of warmth in our hearts. Its seeds are already planted within us in our great capacity for loving. As love opens our hearts and softens our edges, so ultimately do our complimentary words. By giving compliments more frequently and with focus, we reap specific and untold benefits across all of our relationships and our daily ways of going through the world.

If we truly value the idea of raising the tone of the conversation in the world around us, we must begin by conveying the value we find in others in our daily encounters. For a shift to occur in the world, it has to start with us.

Let's delve into this conversation further in order to understand what makes compliments so powerful.

Complimentology Tips

Start small.

You may think only bigger accomplishments deserve compliments, but remember that simple is good; simple is significant and rewarding in its own right. Look around for easy, down-to-earth things about which to share a compliment: how the carpool mom is always on time; how your coworker always remembers to turn off the kitchen light. While these may seem incidental, you don't need to wait for a monumental achievement to share an authentic, kind word of encouragement.

Decide to build the compliment habit.

By now you have no doubt heard that it takes 21 days to make a new habit. Or 30 days, or 15 days. Whichever is correct, the purpose of passing a time hurdle on the road to whatever you want more of is allowing time to "practice, practice, practice." This isn't like forcing yourself to sit at the piano as you did for piano lessons when you were a kid. It's an enjoyable exercise, as people love to get compliments (don't you?). Make it even more enjoyable by sharing your compliments with plenty of smiles and a sense of humor—we all can use more laughter in our lives.

Be relentless in focusing on the good.

Be on the lookout for both little things and big things—to give a compliment on. As you notice the interesting, fun, clever, helpful and positive, you will begin to overlook the frustrating, forgotten, misplaced, and stressful, which will change your outlook and expand your authentic, positive voice and loving presence on this planet. Of course, you need a buddy you can complain with occasionally—but make it an exception, rather than the rule.

Exercise - Count your compliments.

Pick a day, or if you're brave, several days, and start a compliment/complaint tally sheet. The easiest way is to take a piece of paper, draw a line down the middle and put those two words at the top of each column. You could also use the notes section of your phone, the computer or two different-colored sticky notes—whatever works for you.

Over the course of the day or days, try to be as honest and open as you can and make a hash mark for each comment you voice, categorizing it as a compliment, complaint or criticism. Everyone I know who has done this, including me, has found it eye-opening to see how many negative comments they make versus positive ones. Consider when and how you can reverse this tally, one compliment at a time. Remember: slow, steady changes in direction eventually turn the ocean liner.

CHAPTER TWO

Nine Qualities That Make Compliments So Nourishing

There are two ways to spread light:
be the candle or the mirror
that reflects it.

~Edith Wharton

Sometimes our light goes out but is blown
into flame by another being. Each of us
owes deepest thanks to those who
have rekindled this light.

~Albert Schweitzer

uthor, poet and scholar John O'Donahue, in *Anam Cara, A Book of Celtic Wisdom*, describes a way of understanding the soul using "candlelight perception," which is a perfect level of illumination from which to consider the underlying foundation of compliments. As opposed to the glare of a study lamp or an overhead fluorescent bulb, candlelight enhances both the obvious and that which is less visible, blending the foreground and background into one similarly toned scene. Looking at compliments through a candlelight view reveals their more readily apparent practical application as well as their less-visible foundational forces.

In its most understandable aspect, a compliment is a cheerful exchange, a positively vibrating inter-action among people—which often elicits a smile and a sharing of good feelings. The less evident background qualities that a compliment embodies include a number of elementary spiritual and ethical principles and traits. Part of the reason that compliments are so nourishing—soul-satisfying and life changing—is the combination of these qualities in the support, approval and love we send out to others when we give our compliments and that resonate inside of us when we receive them.

Compliments are, in essence, bigger than the sum of their parts. Compliments are none of the following fundamental attributes alone—and yet all of them, at the same time.

ONE - *Generosity*

To be rich in admiration and free from envy, to rejoice greatly in the good of others, to love with such generosity of heart that your love is still a dear possession in absence or unkindness - these are the gifts which money cannot buy.

~ Robert Louis Stevenson

Compliments are a completely generous action. The definition of "generosity" is unselfishness, a willingness to give or share. This is the essence of a compliment. Compliments turn the focus outward, away from what you want and what you need, and yet, interestingly, they also often give you what you want to get. Want to feel more love? Generously give love away.

You never know the extent of the effect of your generous action. Every day we are offered opportunity after opportunity to be generous with compliments in small ways. You might write these off as no big deal, but they are actually more important than you realize. When you offer a simple, generous compliment, you are connecting with another person in a way that creates powerful energy, energy you can use to rock your bit of the world, if you choose.

TWO - *Gratitude*

Gratitude is a duty which ought to be paid, but which none have a right to expect.

~Jean Jacques Rousseau

I don't remember where I first heard the concept of a gratitude journal—from Sarah Ban Breathnach, in *Simple Abundance*? From Oprah?—but many of us have adopted this practice over the years. Besides helping me weather sunny and stormy times alike, using this more active habit of gratitude, rather than taking things for granted, has opened my inner awareness and improved my quality of life. Speaking a language of gratitude nearly guarantees you a more joyous attitude. You set your heart's generators to react positively as you notice and appreciate what is working, rather than life's difficulties.

Sharing a compliment is one sure way of passing that gratitude along and spreading more joy at the same time. I know I often well up with complimentary thoughts when I'm feeling particularly grateful. As I walk the hallways of my kids' schools, wondering how on earth anyone could have the patience to deal with so many kids day in and day out, let alone teach them anything, I feel tremendous gratitude for those who have chosen teaching for their careers. At these times, I get specific when conveying my thanks to my kids' teachers, complimenting them on their creativity, the way they inspired my child with a certain language arts assignment or helped my child gain an appreciation of a particular historical event.

My friend Kristina and her husband both work full-time and have two kids. With such a heavy workload, she decided to hire someone to do the time-consuming job of cleaning the house. She was so happy to be free of this task —at least the big stuff each week—that she often walks through her clean house and then calls to thank her housekeeper. The first time she phoned, the housekeeper responded to her call defensively, obviously thinking there was something wrong that made my friend call her. But when she finally understood that Kristina was calling to thank her, not complain about something, she relaxed and gratefully received the compliment on her job well done.

As Kristina learned, after giving a compliment, you often get a smile or "thank you" in gratitude back from the receiver. This generates another boost of positive energy, further amplifying the compliment's positive effect.

THREE - Acknowledgment

I have yet to find the man, however exalted his station, who did not do better work and put forth greater effort under a spirit of approval than under a spirit of criticism.

~Charles Schwab

Is an accomplishment that goes unrecognized still a success? Of course it is! There are numerous reasons to do the right thing just because it's the right thing to do— without worrying or expecting people to notice.

Similarly, should we always praise simple things done right? No, not always. It's healthier for people to get in the habit of doing the right things without constantly seeking exterior incentives or recognition. But one of the most positive, proven-effective tactics for eliciting certain behavior is to recognize it and praise it. While this praise-the-good, leave-the-bad strategy tends to remind me eerily of pet obedience training, suffice it to say that it far outperforms focusing on the negative when it comes to managing behavior.

The next time you are tempted to remind someone for the umpteenth time that he or she has left the dishes in the sink yet again instead of putting them in the dishwasher, try asking yourself if there would be earthquakes or other earth-shattering consequences if you simply let it go and waited for something to commend instead. While it can feel like it's your job to make sure others know what they're doing wrong, most likely they already know this—and your complaining is more self-serving than you realize, because it comes across as comparing your virtuosity to their ineptitude.

Don't be stingy with praise. Lavish it where it's due, and you'll reap rewards, too, as you continue to share in the joyful feelings your compliments elicit in others.

FOUR - Appreciation

Appreciation is a wonderful thing: It makes what is excellent in others belong to us as well.

~Voltaire

Kim doesn't play a musical instrument, but her children took band class in middle school and learned to play the flute and trumpet. They will never play at Carnegie Hall or even, as it turns out, continue on to high school band. But they started in sixth grade not even knowing how to hold an instrument and progressed to playing recognizable pieces of some length and difficulty. As Kim complimented their beginning notes and then the way they practiced and, finally, how they performed at their concerts, she shared in their achievements and gained tremendous appreciation for their efforts.

Through compliments, we examine more closely that which we experience around us—in our lives and in the bigger world around us. As a result, we develop a keener sense of appreciation for our surroundings. The trend toward a more simple approach to life attests to the fact that in the past few years many of us have developed more nuanced views of all aspects of our busy lifestyles. Giving more and better compliments goes hand-in-hand with this approach, shifting our mindsets to focus more on what is working, not what is missing, and what is important to us, allowing us to sort through the extraneous to find our true sources of joy.

I've realized that sometimes I don't even know the depth of my feelings about a certain topic until I hear myself saying something out loud, answering a question or making a comment. Similarly, sometimes what we compliment helps reveal what we consider important and helps us refine our appreciation of it.

FIVE - *E*steem

People are crying up the rich and variegated plumage of the peacock, and he is himself blushing at the sight of his ugly feet.

~Sa'Di

I mentioned to my sister once that whenever I watched a certain tennis star in a match on television, this player reminded me of her. She was pleased by this observation, more than I expected. She said that no one had ever told her that she might resemble that strong, athletic kind of woman. Since she thought of herself in terms of her intellect, rather than physical prowess, I could see that my comment had opened up a window in her vision of herself to give her yet another view.

Abraham Maslow, in his hierarchy of human development, ranked the need for esteem—a sense of self-worth, confidence, the respect of others—just below the need for love in humans. The act of complimenting lets us participate in the radiance of others by reflecting back to them their unique brilliances, giving them building blocks to their self-esteem.

We have at our center the desire to be seen, a longing to be known—not the "be seen" of having fifteen minutes of fame, but to be recognized for who we are, as our own, special brand of us. Og Mandino wrote in the classic book, *The Greatest Salesman in the World*, "None that came before, none that live today and none that come tomorrow" are the same as anyone else, so each of us is "nature's greatest miracle."

We each long to be recognized, not only for the outward personae that we present to the world on a day-to-day basis, but for our deepest, innermost personhood. This craving is mixed with trepidation: have you experienced a moment of worry or fleeting terror that others, as they got to know the real you, would turn away? I have.

It takes a certain amount of trust to reveal our real selves. Yet, the sorrow of not being seen can leave us paralyzed and lost, and is embedded in many of the heinous actions that make the nightly news.

Since words are the label for ideas, a compliment that highlights someone's uniqueness allows them to hear how much their particular gifts are valued—even for doing nothing but being themselves and, therefore, acknowledging their inherent worth as a human being—and can help fill this deep-rooted longing for esteem that we all have.

As we continue to build our own sense of self worth, we grow in our capacity for kindness and generosity to others. Therefore, as we fill others' cups through genuine compments, we further increase their capacity to compliment others, creating an upward spiral that benefits everyone.

SIX - *Respect*

If we lose love and self respect for each other,
this is how we finally die.

~Maya Angelou

Communicating respect is an important part of recognizing the contributions of people who surround us at all levels of society. Despite our best intentions, many of us tend to pigeon-hole people quickly, based on their looks, their clothes, the cars they drive and other surface factors. When we're judging, we're moving away from an objective appraisal and letting negative emotions, such as fear, envy, and prejudice, get in the way. Criticism, comparisons, labels, put-downs, and insults are all forms of judgment, all ways of saying that another person is "wrong." (Hint: if your first response is, "They should..." or, "You need to...," you are coming first from judgment.)

As we practice respect, we open our hearts to a simple thought: what is it like to be the other person? And that's where compliments come in. To give a compliment, you have to see others with an open mind. This is key to being more objective, to forming a basis of respect and being able to accept differences.

A quick, cordial compliment can help break the momentary barriers around us—in line at the post office, sitting next to a stranger at a school assembly or across the table at a conference. It allows us to remember that we all bring different approaches and gifts to the world, and that we all share more than it might appear from the outside.

By resisting the urge to judge, offering a compliment instead, even something small or obvious, we contribute a vibration of respect to the world and uplift the energy around us. For example, many teenagers may be unfamiliar with what the elders in their neighborhoods or families did in their yesterdays—or even do today. And many seniors today tend to lump teens into categories based on what they think of "young people" in general. By complimenting one another, they actually have to find something to recognize, and that requires taking a closer look. This ultimately conveys a sense of respect for the other person, a sense that that person is worth the time it takes to make the observation.

When my mother compliments my son for his hard work in school, she conveys respect for his effort and for him, while he can feel part of something bigger, a generational passing of the baton of respect. When my daughter compliments my mother's quilt-making prowess, she is recognizing this skill honed with dedication and love over years. Even if it's not her taste or favorite style, she shows her respect for grandma's abilities.

SEVEN - Hope

Hope arouses, as nothing else can arouse,
a passion for the possible.

~William Sloan Coffin

Compliments offer an element of hope, the unexpressed combination of inspiration and expectation that looks for the good in people instead of complaining about the bad. It particularly comes into play when you're in difficult situations or with difficult people: someone, perhaps, who irritates you; a situation in which you feel powerless or perhaps when you know others feel "less than," for some reason—in the past you were the room-mother or keynote presenter and they think you've got all the knowledge. How can you impart hope to them?

Online marketing expert Laura Roeder teaches technology to entrepreneurs. A recent email message of hers sported the following subject line: "Well, hello there good looking!" She says she uses this quick, fun compliment as a simple way to give encouragement to business owners who may have "previously felt too daunted to even get started." Perhaps this compliment sparks a sense of hope in the recipient, making the idea of high-tech training less intimidating. "I want to get them started with a smile and ease any fear that they might be feeling," Laura says.

What about someone who rarely remembers to do what you asked of them around the house or lets others pick up the slack at the office? It's easy to simply give up and focus on the negative. But searching out something about them to compliment helps switch the feeling from powerlessness to hopefulness. Your compliment has the potential to generate even a small sense of accomplishment in them that might translate into different behavior into the future—the feeling that not all hope is lost in their behavior! In this way, compliments can give you control over difficult people and situations and offer optimism for the future.

EIGHT - *Acceptance*

*The curious paradox is that when I accept myself
just as I am, then I can change.*

~Carl Rogers

In the past, I fought the idea that contentment is a premise of happiness. After all, if you are content with how things are, doesn't that imply a kind of giving up? If you accept where you are in life, doesn't that mean that you are no longer moving forward? Yet the reality is that acceptance brings the understanding that this moment is the highest and best place for you at this time. In acceptance of others, we find so much more freedom to be ourselves along the way.

I remember hearing this expressed so well by Oprah some time ago and being impressed with her thoughts about not looking back in regret at what you did at some former time or in some past experience. At those times, she reasoned, you were acting at your most capable, or even simply as the most fully expressed you that you had reached up to that point. Therefore, you should accept what you did with grace and humility, hopefully recognizing that you have learned and grown since then.

A compliment is part of that kind of acceptance, both for you and for others. It strengthens whichever rung we're standing on in life's ladder. By complimenting someone, we offer them the gift of our acceptance of where they are at that moment. Will they take another step up that ladder, beyond what we've praised? Perhaps. But we've contributed to the sturdy place in which they find themselves today. They experience even a moment of acceptance for exactly who they are and where they are in life right now. As in Carl Rogers' quote above, by accepting (in a compliment) rather than opposing (in a criticism), we are allowing someone the grace and the space to own where they are, as well as the space from which to move up, if necessary.

NINE - Paying it Forward

Just concentrate on helping one person, giving hope to one person, and that person in turn may give hope to somebody else and it will spread out.

~Aaron Abrahamsen

Beyond the previously mentioned enduring and layered aspects of compliments is the concept that, when you compliment someone, you are wrapping up all of these qualities and giving them away, delivering to others a powerful gift into which they can delve to continue this kind approach that changes the world at the most personal level: individual to individual, moment to moment. In the multi-faceted compliment, then, is the essence of paying it forward.

When you compliment, you pass along to another this combination of powerful virtues with the deep warmth of your heart, which you tap into at the moment of the compliment. When someone receives a compliment, it often fires up a compliment from them to someone else, as if passing the Olympic torch to the next runner.

The forward spark of kindness is the subject of the novel and subsequent movie *Pay It Forward* (Catherine Ryan Hyde; Warner Bros. Pictures, 2000). In response to a class assignment to think of a way to change the world, Trevor (played by Haley Joel Osment) creates a plan to do favors for people – but with a twist: he asks that they not pay back the favors, but instead pay them forward.

Trevor explains his mathematical calculation that proves that doing something nice for three people will create an exponential movement of good deeds that could change the world. I won't reveal the ending for those of you who haven't seen the movie. Suffice it to say that, as this boy begins to enact his three acts of paying it forward, he chooses to ignore people's faults or what's wrong and focuses on uplifting others, keeping simple kindness and generosity in mind. Compliments are a perfect example of this forward orientation; when giving a sincere compliment, we don't expect to get one back. We have shined a ray of light on how small an act feeds someone's dampened spirits and sparks their darkened light.

Even the advertising world drew on this pay-kindness-forward concept in an insurance company commercial that garnered a lot of attention when it ran on TV and later on YouTube (http://www.youtube.com/watch?v=wMwoexR1evo). In this beautifully soundtracked scenario ("Half Acre," by Hem), people who merely witness someone else do a good deed are inspired to perform their own acts of kindness later for someone else: the woman who sees a man rescue a toy fallen from a stroller later saves a coffee cup from falling off a table, which is seen by a man who later helps a person who has slipped on the sidewalk, which is seen by a man who later holds an elevator door open for someone, and so on. While the final person in the commercial witnessing the good deed is the same first person we saw rescuing the child's dropped toy (which we realize is impossible in real life), the message resounds because it is so clear: one single, generous act of kindness can ripple forward, making a bigger impact on all of us.

Taking an extra, considerate step is valuable, regardless of any return benefit, yet we often underestimate what even the smallest demonstration of caring can do for another. These examples of paying forward may be a novel's storyline and a Madison Avenue scenario; yet in reality, we may never know what disappointment we soothe, fear we assuage or other compliment we inspire by passing the compliment baton to others around us. Which person's actions do you know that you overlook or dismiss? Who might be waiting for a bit of praise? Which child, spouse or sister is feeling taken for granted? This is where the energy and might of a single compliment contributes to the progress of our human development, to the very healing needed around us.

Before we get to the specific ways to use compliments as one multi-functional tool, like a trusty, multi-function Swiss Army knife—a tool that can lift your spirits, deepen your relationships and help uplift the world around you—let's examine in the next chapter how they work and what makes them so powerful.

Complimentology Tips

Think gratitude.

If you are having trouble thinking about how you'll give more compliments, start with grateful thoughts first. Count your blessings, even if you have to focus on being thankful for what you've escaped instead of what you've achieved.

When I am in serious need of motivation, I supersaturate. I'm doing my morning prayers, meditating, putting up Post-It note affirmations on the kitchen cabinets, writing on the bathroom mirror. Begin your own super-gratitude saturation for inspiration: make a list of 100 things to be thankful for. Surely many compliments to others will be revealed in all that gratitude. Stop focusing on yourself, and look outward. This is one of the secrets of life.

Compliment even when you're not really in the mood.

Do you think you need to be feeling especially inspired to compliment others? If so, you might miss too many opportunities to make a difference. Based on the fake-it-'til-you-make-it theory of getting ahead, act as if you are charming and courteous, even when you're not feeling so, and complimenting will become easier. This isn't being disingenuous; it is tapping into your inner firelight that's there all the time, whether you acknowledge it or not, and lighting other's torches from it.

Get inspiration from your own experience.

Improve your compliments by getting in touch with what it feels like for you in the giving and receiving process of compliments.

When you receive a compliment, stop and note how it makes you feel, what emotions you experience, what thoughts it brings up. Focus on the feelings of well-being, and let them really sink in.

Similarly, when you are giving compliments, take note of how it feels when you give them and how the recipients react. Check back with these feelings as you keep complimenting to deepen your understanding of how giving compliments improves the energy and atmosphere for both the giver and receiver.

Think of compliments as a gift.

You don't have to be an extrovert or an expert to add the powerful, practical tool of complimenting to your life-enhancing cache. Consider it as an act as simple as giving a gift. Think about it – we even say to "give" a compliment. Giving is powerful; it is an outflow of love in all forms, and giving of yourself in a compliment is among the greatest and easiest demonstrations of love. Give knowing you don't need anything, not even validation, back. And easiest of all, give yourself compliments, often.

Dig into the compliment why.

If compliments seem too small to make a difference, re-connect with your desire to be of service. If you truly want to make a difference in the world, rely on that desire to open yourself up to spreading more praise and recognition. Remember: making changes in the world starts with you. Compliments are but one small tool in your cache of ways to contribute to the greater good. As attributed to Mother Teresa, "There are no great things, only small things with great love."

CHAPTER THREE

Eight Ways Compliments Are More Powerful Than You Think

Appreciative words are the most powerful force for good will on earth.

~Dr. George Crane

he words "compliment" and "powerful" don't seem to belong together. When you think of compliments, maybe you always pictured something courteous and mannerly. Cultured? Yes. But powerful? I'm going to show you how, like Scarlet O'Hara, who transformed herself from genteel to influential and commanding, compliments can also do heavy lifting.

No, compliments won't stave off natural disasters or global dilemmas. In fact, they aren't even appropriate in all situations. And after reaching out with a compliment, you may have to exit-stage-left so someone else's bad attitude doesn't pull you down. But compliments are a more powerful method than you may have ever realized or understood to switch on the light of your highest self, the brilliance of your relationships and your joyful life—and be a light for someone else along the way.

Here are eight ways compliments are more powerful than you realized:

ONE

Compliments enlist the power of language.
Words are powerful. Even if Language Arts Class wasn't your strong suit in school, there is no doubt that language is among the most dominant influences in our society.

In Earl Nightingale's classic *Lead the Field* program, he details research that identifies one of the singular distinctions among the most successful people: their use of language. In other words, it's not simply education or background or other circumstances that allows a person to gain influence, but their mastery over language. This puts words right at the top of the power that's available to us.

By using the right appreciative words and phrases, we have the ability to influence the outcome of a student's work, enlist a spouse's cooperation, or even inspire a co-worker to shoulder their responsibility. That's heavy lifting on the part of well-chosen vowels and consonants!

Is it coincidence that women have long relied on this in their corners of the world? How many stories are told about moms not allowing bad language around their homes? At 82, the father of one of my girlfriends told me that after he returned from serving as a Marine in bloody battles in the Pacific during WWII, his mother said she'd never tolerated "cuss" words before and wouldn't still. He never swore in front of her again.

When my kids were young, they protested our household rule against using the words "stupid" and "hate." "Everyone says them!" they'd wail. Later, they admitted how they began to understand how some words just shouldn't be used no matter what others may do.

We readily accept that some words are unacceptable in civilized society and understand how they've been used over the ages to belittle and humiliate. Degradation and insults can negatively impact people long into adulthood, despite the "sticks and stones" rhyme we repeat to our kids.

So, in understanding the negative power that words can have, we find the positive power of language, too. Words may have limitations when it comes to communicating our thoughts, but it's important to remember that word choices matter and language itself is powerful.

On top of that, positive words have an energy associated with them, an actual vibrational lift to them. A compliment is a translation of a divine-level thought into words, and as we bless others with a supportive comment or reply, we also bless and allow ourselves to share the same bounty. With their upbeat tone, the complimentary words themselves bring about expansiveness, an enhanced connection that is beneficial to the person saying them, as well as to the one hearing them.

TWO

Compliments refocus our lens. In his book, *Anam Cara*, John O'Donahue states that, "When we are familiar with something, we lose the energy, the edge, and excitement of it." And what breeds more familiarity than our day-to-day relationships with siblings and spouses? Taking others for granted is a slow, insidious phenomenon that exacts tolls on those relationships.

In the case of marriage, for example, taking for granted the very person you love and trust most creates a numbing effect that can permeate the entire relationship. Feeling unappreciated and even underappreciated can evoke slowly simmering emotions that irreparably harm a relationship over time.

"Friendships and relationships suffer immense numbing through the mechanism of familiarization," O'Donahue writes. He goes on to note that, in fact, familiarity is actually a façade—that in our desire to more easily understand others— and control them— we overlook many qualities they might possess that don't fit into our set picture of that person. Ultimately, the least loving thing we can do is to act as if we completely know them and that there is nothing left to learn or see anew.

By undertaking a regular search for something to compliment in our so-very-familiar partner, sister or best friend, we raise the curtain of this façade in order to look beyond the well-known and see with new eyes. With the refocused lens of a compliment, we're able to see "like new," striking at the heart of relationship-weariness and monotony and strengthening our bond.

In *A Return to Love*, Marianne Williamson guides us through a similar thought process about what it means to know someone—and to love them. We may think that until we know someone, we won't know if they are worthy of our love, but she emphasizes the opposite, that until we love someone, we'll never know them. "We hold ourselves separate from people and wait for them to earn our love," Williamson writes.

Stopping to look through the eyes of love, when considering something to compliment, leads us to love first— or to remind ourselves of the deep love that existed before the familiarity of the relationship set in. By taking the time to notice, for example, that your husband always fills your coffee cup before he fills his—and then voicing that observation in a compliment—you change your view of your husband from the guy who always leaves plates in the sink or crumbs on the counter. By refocusing your lens, you come to see him in a new light. Through compliments, especially more precise and explicit compliments, we take the time to acknowledge others, to see them, to reflect back to them their most brilliant selves and to hold precious, for however short a time, that part of them that is unique and perfect exactly as it is.

The lowly compliment opens the heart of the giver, softening her outlook, expanding her patience and enhancing her understanding of others, *and* uplifts the recipient, inspiring a burst of pride and swell of happiness in receiving the acknowledgment. The two are joined in a compliment moment, a moment of seeing and being seen, of genuine connection and love. The benefits of this simple interaction spill over into other facets of each person's life, building self-esteem and respect, consideration and tolerance.

THREE

Compliments grow positive change. Many philosophers have articulated the powerful idea that whatever we think about we become. Another way of putting this is: *whatever you say, stays. Or: whatever you think you know, grows.*

How easy is it to get all wrapped up in what's not working! I know I would often decide, as I said prayers, meditated or waited for the teapot to boil each morning, to focus only on the good with my children. "See the best, leave the rest," I'd remind myself. Often, we weren't all out the door before I'd brought up something someone *hadn't* done. ("You didn't turn the light off in your closet – again!"). Of course, this last-minute complaining never helped them change. Instead, it added to everyone's irritation and left my implication of my child's worthlessness in both of our minds, setting up a negative start to the day.

The simplest of facts is that people choose to live up to our vision of them by consciously or subconsciously adopting our perception of them. We must be careful of the words we wield, as this kind of negativity is such a strong sword!

If we compliment someone, we're expanding the vision of how they feel perceived, and we help them grow into that vision. We are, in essence, rewriting the story of our relationship.

In giving more frequent and specific compliments that focus on the good outcome—the right behavior or better attitude (even if those qualities are displayed less frequently)—you don't validate the behavior you're ignoring. Instead, you open up the space for positive growth. This isn't simply for the good of the other person. It strongly benefits both of you as you raise the vibration of your relationship, your family, and the planet.

FOUR

Compliments are taking control. In giving a compliment, you jump into the driver's seat and take off. What a relief—and what power! As busy women, we're often at the mercy of others. How often do you get to do exactly what you want, without negotiating it (think of your work situation or even simply trying to get all your family members ready to go with you for a mere trip to the store)?

In giving a compliment, you don't have to consult or discuss or come to consensus. You are in creative control. What you draw on for the compliment, the words you choose, even the timing—it's all up to you.

The momentum of doing this yourself creates an uplifting energy and helps ameliorate feelings of powerlessness in a situation. For instance, when waiting in line somewhere, how many of us feel helpless and frustrated—powerless to move along faster, powerless to leave, since we have to stay there to get what we need done? But by finding a way to connect with the service person or others around you through a simple compliment, you immediately take back some of your power in the situation.

Friend and business owner Jamie Wallace used this power recently when she came across a harried, grumpy woman next to her at the deli counter. "Instead of feeding into her bad mood, I complimented her on her earrings. She absolutely lit up and told me how she bought them on vacation in New Mexico last year. Her whole demeanor and energy changed," Jamie said.

Jamie admitted that she wasn't trying to start a relationship with the woman. She simply jumped in to take some control of the situation. "I hope I had a positive impact on her day."

It may seem like a small way to get involved and take control, but everything is put together brick by brick, and your individual compliments are building blocks that create a worthy life.

FIVE

Compliments are active. Thinking, studying and planning are important in life, but they only go so far. It's critical to finally act. (Consider the saying "if wishes were horses," which posits that if all we had to do were wish, we'd all be thinner, smarter or richer—or whatever our secret desires are!)

Having a positive thought about someone or thinking positively about a specific outcome is important. But combining the thought with action tips the scales to a positive outcome. That thought you are thinking can only be born through the actions you take. In giving a compliment, you've chosen to not leave the opportunity on the table or let it slip by.

Entrepreneur Michael Masterson titled one of his recent books, *Ready, Fire, Aim,* to illustrate how best to launch a business. The title implies how successful business people should get prepared but quickly take action, then adjust and fire away again. As you'll learn later, the best compliments work through their specificity and authenticity; but when complimenting others, it's a waste of precious moments to worry about getting it right all the time. By taking the many opportunities to compliment that come your way, you soon figure out what style of complimenting works best and increase your desire and ability to praise more frequently.

Popular self-help author and business mentor Dr. Joe Vitale asserts that taking inspired action is a crucial step on the path to abundance and success. Giving a compliment inspired by a friend or loved one is at its profound best an inspired action of the heart, and it will return to you an abundance of your own joyful feeling.

SIX

Compliments yield accomplishment. By giving a compliment, you build your own sense of actually getting something done. Again, you're not building a public monument or signing a world peace accord. Even so, compliments can help chip away at your sense that you're spinning your wheels at best and falling behind at worst.

With all of the things on your plate that are often left undone as you move from one day's to-do-list to another's, you can accomplish a small-but-great thing by taking the opportunity to give a heartfelt compliment. If you have ever asked, "What can one person do?" this is part of the answer. Just think of how many times you don't say anything, leaving a host of un-acted-upon opportunities around you.

Giving a compliment takes attention and a little time but yields a strong sense that, in the midst of all you have on your plate, you got something done. You may not have cooked that wonderful home-made meal you promised yourself you would prepare—that is, before you got stuck in traffic after the football game or recital—but you took advantage of the opportunity to tell the other mom watching the game or recital alongside you that she looked great today. And that's an important achievement in spreading love.

SEVEN

Compliments are long lasting. Wrapping something in emotion virtually guarantees its longevity, and as compliments both begin in emotion and elicit emotion, they become part of our active and cellular memory.

The infusion of memories with emotion has been linked to our evolution. From the beginning, human survival depended on learning through trial-and-error behavior. As humans experienced intense emotions from life-and-death situations, what worked (yielding happiness, relief) and what didn't (creating fear, anger) became more thoroughly embedded in our collective brains because of those associated emotions.

Many psychological investigations have shown that emotion has a powerful impact on what we remember. Try this often-quoted experiment: remember where you were or what you were doing when you first heard about the terror attacks on 9/11. Most people can, almost to the minute they heard the news. That is because they were stunned, horrified, fearful.

Put into the positive, remember how you felt when you said "I do." Or landed your dream job. Or when you first held your new baby—or sent your son or daughter off to college. Scientists have researched how emotional stimuli boost memory by activating neuro-chemical activity in the parts of the brain where we encode and recall.

All compliments certainly don't elicit the emotional content of such momentous, life-changing situations. But the best compliments, the most unexpected and uplifting compliments, benefit both the receiver and the giver long after they've been voiced. Compliments are inherently heart-based, and even the most casual of compliments can provide an immediate emotional jumpstart in those neurons in our brains.

EIGHT

Compliments contribute to your own success.
When you actively compliment those around you, you not only highlight them, but you stand out in the process, too. My girlfriend Happy used to say that someone who asked you out on a date had already demonstrated a positive trait by having the good sense to pick you to ask out! As it turns out, researchers say that we're biologically primed to prefer those who seem to be interested in us.

While the key to the very best compliments is to make appreciative comments that won't benefit you back, the cumulative effect of those generous, authentic compliments is to raise your visibility to the person you praised. By looking for the good in others and expressing it constructively, you build more trusting and successful relationships. This is the true route to gaining popularity and influence! By giving people more than they expect, you always get back more than you give.

Who can't picture the people everyone likes when they walk in the room—the persons we always want to work with or help out? Usually, these people are perceived as charming, and the truth is that it's because they focus on others. After all, it's the givers that get, not the takers. If you doubt this propensity to focus on others being associated with success, the next time you have the opportunity to be in the room with a business or civic leader, you may observe how they often compliment someone with others nearby to hear the praise, further spreading the effect of the kind words.

While offering insincere praise to others will rapidly cancel out any goodwill you hope to create, it's not too farfetched to say that compliments can bring you a better income or a better intimate relationship. These results don't come only from the compliments, but also by creating long-lasting, positive impressions about you in others' minds. This ultimately contributes to your own success. Now that you've learned the power of complimenting, let's take a look next at what actually constitutes a compliment.

Complimentology Tips

Take regular compliment action.

Nothing succeeds like success, so the more frequently you flex your compliment muscle, the more habitual you will make giving compliments and the more you will continuously manifest more joy in your life and around you. I have found that I have to promise myself I won't quit for the first three days of nearly any new thing I am doing in which I really want to succeed. Ever try to lose weight? For me, the best way to actually stick to a weight-loss plan is to lose some weight in the first days, because it is actually only in achieving some success that I get inspired to keep going. Those times I succeeded in staying with an exercise plan or eating more healthily were *after* I had succeeded for a few days first. And until I know I can count on myself for those first days of success, I don't even try any more.

So when raising your compliment quotient, try to get several days of success in a row under your belt. Maybe start with your family or spouse when going on a trip or vacation. The change of scenery, lack of having other things on your to-do list, or break in routine, can create the beginning of a space for you to lavish on the praise and let the rest fade away. After this success, you can continue to build a compliment focus when you get back home.

Take control of out-of-control complaining.

Have you been feeling frustrated by a family member and voicing those feelings routinely? Think of what would happen if you just kept quiet and took care not to say anything bad (as many of us were instructed when we were young)? All humans desire to get better, to be more; it's a natural, deep-seated drive. By not giving voice to the negative, you are taking control of the situation by removing yourself as the victim in your previous version of the relationship and taking yourself out of that drama. And, importantly, you are giving the other person a vision of the better person they could be.

Act like a celebrity—the good kind.

In our star-struck culture where celebrities are often perceived as the "bad girls and boys," such as Paris Hilton or Russell Crowe, it's still true that many of the most popular celebrities and prominent public figures are also those most beloved. Why? Because they are consistently gracious and generous, highlighting, for example, how great it was to work with others on a movie set or noting that their accomplishment was part of a team effort. Take a cue from perennial favorites like Tom Hanks, Diane Lane, Chris O'Donnell, or Sandra Bullock and gain more acclaim by demonstrating a true interest in others through your compliments. Take a "Look at you!" approach to others instead of being a "Look at me" bore. Remember that everyone wants esteem and appreciation. So when you regularly remember to reflect back to others what's positive about them, you can't help but shine brighter yourself.

Wrap your compliment with emotion.

Just as body language can give a different impression from your words if the two don't match up, the emotion you put into a compliment can change its impact as well. Remember: everything wrapped with emotion is longer lasting, with more impact, so you might as well not try to praise someone if you are going to deliver a monotone, half-hearted compliment. It may even backfire. Try to get the complete attention of the person you're acknowledging. Give the compliment when looking into their eyes, and say it with conviction, as in: "You have been doing an exceptional job. You take risks and take the lead instead of hanging back. I admire you greatly."

Name drop.

For a success boost from your compliment, add in the recipient's name, too. "You look fantastic today, Susan!" Research shows that when people hear their names, certain "reward centers" in their brains light up, which makes your compliment even more effective at raising their vibration as well as make them think highly of you for it. But do not overdo this—saying their name over and again comes across unnaturally and sounds false, negating the positive effect of your compliment.

SECTION TWO

DISSECTING THE COMPLIMENT QUOTIENT

CHAPTER FOUR

What Is—and Isn't— a Compliment?

Sticks and stones are hard on bones
Aimed with angry art,
Words can sting like anything
But silence breaks the heart.

~Phyllis McGinley,
"Ballade of Lost Objects," 1954

ebster's defines a compliment as an *"expression of admiration."* Simply, any combination of words used to highlight something in a way that honors or pays tribute to someone adds up to a compliment. These expressions are amplified versions of being nice, but are more than merely being polite. It takes an active effort to go that extra mile to articulate these thoughts.

While the dictionary definition works as a broad look at what makes up a compliment, compliments also come in many more nuanced packages. Let's take a bit more in-depth look at the compliment and its relatives—including a few of the troublesome ones.

Compliment or Complement?

If you're not a word aficionado, as I am, you might get tripped up by these two different words often used erroneously for each other: "compliment" and "complement." We've been talking about the definition of "compliment," which can be used as a noun or verb, as in "Give a compliment" or the act of complimenting. But the word "complement" has a different meaning. It indicates that which "completes, fills or brings to perfection." And it, too, can be used as a noun or verb. An example is, "Her hearty way of laughing was the perfect complement to her husband's sense of humor." Or, "The necklace complemented her sweater as it highlighted the variations in the color of the yarn." While it can be a little tricky, the good news is that when you use it in conversation, no one will be the wiser! Just pay attention when you use it in writing.

—*Praise*

Praise is a compliment of recognition, a statement acknowledging something well done, a way in which we express approval. Giving praise is an integral part of good parenting and working relations and shouldn't be saved just for those occasions when we're trying to reinforce behavior.

—*Congratulations*

The word "congratulate" comes from Latin, *congratulari*, meaning "to wish joy" (don't you love this?) . We often reserve this word for something that has taken a long period of time to achieve, such as graduation, wedding anniversary, new job, or a new baby.

But we can express a hearty "congratulations!" for many types of accomplishments. We can use this 'wishing joy' word whenever someone undertakes learning and mastering something new. Any time someone has tried learning anything new, they're avoiding stagnation and often conquering some kind of fear. They therefore deserve admiration. Kids particularly relish this type of compliment, as they've often heard it bandied about in adult circles.

How a Compliment Helps Your Heart

When you compliment others in celebration of something accomplished – in other words, in congratulations—you are actually helping your heart. Reports of recent research show that expressing your joyful enthusiasm can help keep your heart disease-free. For instance, a 10-year study linked people who scored high on joy and enthusiasm with a lower incidence of heart disease compared to those who experienced those positive emotions less often. Also, constant high levels of stress-induced cortisol are linked to higher incidence of high blood pressure and diabetes. These healthful findings are all the more reason to look at sharing congratulations and compliments as part of a relaxing, stress-busting routine. So take a break to celebrate someone else's accomplishment and help your heart, too!

—*Flattery*

To *flatter* someone is to make a complimentary remark. We usually consider it to be a flattering compliment when we praise someone's looks or comment on a person's talent.

Unfortunately, because it can be taken way beyond social bounds and good taste, flattery has gotten a bad rap—a sad result, perhaps, of political correctness in the office place? But when we flatter someone such as our spouse, we're simply engaging in the old-school practice of sweet-talk. There's a reason it's called *sweet* talk—

just as there's a reason for the phrase, *"you catch more flies with honey than vinegar."* Sprinkling simple, sweet, flattering words around adds a delicious warmth to our day-to-day interactions. It opens our hearts to giving and expressing love, and, let's face it, is simply delicious!

—Thank yous

Oddly enough, we often withhold our compliments from those whose services we pay for. Is it because we think since we're paying them we don't have to recognize the level of expertise done on our behalf?

My friend Joy has been successfully self-employed for years, yet she knows that taxes and keeping the books are not her specialty. So she uses an accountant to do this for her. "When I picked up my finished tax return, I told him what an excellent job he does and how much I appreciated all his work on my behalf, how he really knows his stuff," she related to me. As they talked further, he told her that he doesn't hear compliments from his clients very often, and how great it was,

Give 'Em A Hand

While it's impossible to pinpoint an exact origin of the practice of clapping to indicate praise, *Take Our Word For It* website notes that the tradition has been around since at least the Middle Ages. Early mentions of applause coincide with the beginning of public performances. The custom may be even older than that. Some sources claim the Romans used a ritual of applause for public performances, expressing degrees of approval through the length and loudness of the clapping. In some instances, it's noted that they snapped fingers, instead, or clapped with a flat palm.

especially during this busy season with people literally demanding the impossible, to hear her kind and generous words. When a "thank you" is offered with some elaboration—specific detail about what the person giving the thanks appreciated—it acts as a strong and meaningful compliment.

—Applause

Applause is a familiar way of offering group praise. The louder and longer the applause, the stronger the approval and the greater the collective "compliment." Even the youngest of children love to clap hands, and some say it's an instinctual way to express joy. (Love the joy sharing!)

When is a compliment not?

Those of us who have been in the work force a long time have had more exposure (pun not intended!) to instances of social intimidation if not outright sexual harassment, along the spectrum of having endured leering glances, suggestive talk and, at times, even more blatant and degrading behavior. There is a clear difference between an honest compliment and this kind of either flat-out rudeness, obliviousness to common decency, or the crime of harassment.

For instance, have you encountered the Smooth Talker? This person delivers rapid-fire, clichéd compliments that may catch us off guard, and at first we're pleased to hear them (remember, we don't get many compliments). But as we listen, these gushing compliments start to ring hollow to our ears. Our initial interest becomes feigned interest, and then forced politeness. Ultimately, the attempt to "compliment" has backfired on the poor person, who doesn't realize—or simply doesn't care—that we came to disbelieve nearly everything being said, because they were empty comments.

Someone who immediately crosses the line of decency—often a person more interested in impressing their friends rather than delivering a genuine compliment—is easier to summarily dismiss. Both, however, are people who engage in the unwelcome and counterproductive practice of handing out empty flattery.

Empty flattery is the opposite of complimenting. If, instead of having something genuine to compliment, someone simply gives a very generic or vague compliment, the praise falls flat. Similarly, if someone piles on compliments when one timely or specific comment would have sufficed, they come across as insincere and can undo any good the compliments may have brought initially.

Lisa, an author, editor and writing coach, was approached by someone who said they thought so well of Lisa's writing and had learned so much from it, perhaps she would write a review for their book. When Lisa dug just a

Colorful Comments

Discussing the terms for those who seek favor through a fawning compliment ("brown nose," "kiss ass," etc.), I was struck with the graphic nature of their origins. Despite the vivid picture painted by their "etymological" meaning, people don't seem to think of these terms in such a vulgar way. We do feel, however, their offensive effect when someone is trying to gain favor by giving false compliments and being ingratiating and obsequious. By the way, slightly less vulgarly, you can also be "kowtowing," "backslapping," and "apple polishing" in your "buttering up." And just for the information of you lovers of language: those crude-sounding terms can be used as nouns or verbs.

little deeper, it became apparent that this person was not familiar with Lisa's writing and had, instead, cast a wide net filled with false compliments, trying to reel in some reviews for her book.

The positive lift Lisa had felt from the initial compliments was quickly replaced with disdain for the person, leaving a negative taste in her mouth, perhaps to the detriment of someone else who expresses sincere appreciation of her work in the future.

Empty flattery, in fact, does the opposite of its intent: rather than making someone feel good about a compliment, it leaves that person feeling used and manipulated.

Here are other examples of statements that may, at first, appear to be compliments, but actually work in the opposite way.

—Sucking up

There is a fine line between giving compliments and trying to curry favor with someone—so much so that some people don't even venture into the realm of praise, fearing their intentions will be misunderstood. The terms "butter up," "brown nose," "suck up," and "kiss ass," are all slang expressions describing compliments that have gone too far or are insincere and given for the wrong reasons.

Sucking up is often done in an attempt to keep the peace—to placate a demanding boss or client. A lot of us are guilty of this seemingly harmless way of agreeing or saying something nice for security's sake. Again, there can be a fine line here if you are truly highlighting something good about a person who also happens to have a lot of undesirable characteristics. After all, we've already discussed the fact that what you focus on helps others grow into this better vision of themselves and, maybe, better behavior.

So all compliments given to someone disagreeable may not be brown-nosing. But when a compliment is given strictly to advance oneself, this is the most disingenuous reason to say admiring things, and it is an offensive use of a compliment.

—Sarcastic comments

Worse than sucking up is when the underlying reason for delivering the compliment is either veiled insincerity or sarcasm. Trying to hide disdain in a false compliment is as bad as outright ridicule. Let's face it, usually both the giver and receiver are well aware of the intent of the comment. Jean, for example, had a friend who was keen on giving these kinds of false compliments. The friend would very loudly tell someone passing by, "nice outfit," but more quietly, so that only her friends could hear, she would add, "not." Of course, everyone in earshot of the negating comment would laugh, but somewhere inside they knew that they might be the next victim of this phony complimenter.

—The backhand (and I'm not talking tennis)

You may have heard the phrase "backhanded compliment." This is actually different than a snide or sarcastic comment. Often this disingenuous comment starts out with the essence of a compliment but continues long enough to reveal a somewhat-veiled insult inside. Surely you know these add-on compliment-wreckers:

"You look great today *for your age.*"

"You did a great job *for someone with your skills.*"

"You remembered to clean up the kitchen *this time.*"

Occasionally it can work to give praise in a roundabout or reverse way—but only if you know someone well enough that they understand your sense of humor and perhaps can see the smile on your face. When I was growing up, my father often gave us kids a roundabout compliment. With a twinkle in his eye, he would survey your work, pat you on the shoulder, and just when you expected to hear, "Good job," would say, "It looks like you'll have to do it all over again." You would turn your head and see his smile and immediately understand that this was his praise in fact. (His light-hearted comments weren't always well received by his children, who occasionally forgot their *own* senses of humor!)

Despite the indirectness of these comments from my father, I came to understand that they represented more positive reinforcement than he had received in his youth, and that they were his own brand of loving encouragement, of giving an "atta girl" in his unique style. As my kids started getting older, I noticed that I, too, began occasionally throwing in these more indirect forms of praise, trying to help hone their senses of humor—the legacy of years of training with my father!

Difference between the sexes

Perhaps my father related in this more "backhanded" way because he worked largely in the world of men. Through the years I often wondered how long it took each of the younger workers assigned to learn with him to catch on to his style. They would have simply had no choice in the long run except to understand his "gentle giant" way of communicating his praise. Men do seem to excel at this kind of compliment, and it can be the only form of praise they share with other guys.

"Sure, guys compliment each other, but a lot of times we hide it a bit," says my friend John. "You won't hear us go on and on, but we might simply say, 'nice coat,' when someone we work with walks in." But he also admits they might end up saying something in a more comical way, like adopting a Monty-Python-esque accent and delivering a slightly-disguised-as-sarcasm compliment, such as "you're looking particularly fetching today," instead.

Hang around a group of males and it's not long before you hear the exact opposite of compliments, often with an assortment of colorful language, too. Simply listen to those derisive or mocking comments thrown around during a round of golf or a basketball game, and you're likely to wonder how and why they ever got together to play in the first place or how they stand each other's company.

But they assure those of us on the outside that they wouldn't have it any other way. They know that this is often when and how they're actually getting compliments from other guys.

This use of backhandedness and sarcasm at times can make the gulf between the sexes a little—maybe *a lot*—harder to bridge, especially since women instinctively seek to build relationships and community and, therefore, don't often take the

Late Night Laughs

On a recent night-time talk show, the host and his newly seated guest began engaging in a round of compliments on each other's recent work. Was it simply because the male host and the male guest were getting too emotionally intimate that they soon ended up having a laugh at each other's expense? Or was the decline into sarcasm simply in the name of comedy? Since I can rarely keep my eyes open that late—or because it's a question about the mystery of the male psyche—we may never know.

backhanded route, unless being intentionally hurtful, of course.

Of course, women do have a sense of humor that we use with each other and with our guys, and we can tease others, too. But we don't always understand the sort of banter that men use. We might do well to take a cue from men and be sure to include light-heartedness in the way we acknowledge others. And men could use the reminder to be sure to give some compliments with loving sincerity.

So let's move on to a look at what makes the best, most meaningful and most effective compliments.

Complimentology Tips

Use a motive-meter.

The next time you're around someone "higher up" than you (your boss, or your boss's boss – or even the neighbor who runs the architectural control committee that approves changes in your landscaping), stop before you compliment. Run that compliment—about their new car or jogging outfit—through a motive-meter in your head and heart. If you stand to benefit from your compliment, then maybe you've moved from the praise and into the "butter-up" category. (You know what I mean.) On the other hand, if your comment passes this quick motive check, go ahead and give the compliment and honor your true intentions to recognize or be grateful.

Ramp up real compliments.

Giving genuine compliments is part of an appealing approach that makes people want to be around you. Since the majority of personal success comes through our relationships, those who develop charismatic characteristics often succeed more readily. While complainers are often heard loudest, those with more positive personalities are most sought out, as everyone—even the Negative Nells—wants the support and sanctuary they feel in a charismatic person's presence.

Lighten up.

While men and women may have different approaches to communicating, both sexes love to laugh. Women often note that one of the things they want most in a partner is a sense of humor. And humor is something a lot of men excel at (telling all those jokes you've already forgotten!). Take a hint from presenters and leaders who use laughter to warm up the audience and offer some of your compliments in a more light, engaging way. For example, if your spouse is a football fan, you could tell him he's "the quarterback of my heart" when he makes a call for which restaurant to go to one night and add that you appreciate him taking charge of it; or you might tell your young child who helps clean up he or she is "helpful as a busy bee buzzing around the flowers" and then doing a "buzzing bee" dance or impersonation with them.

Compliment to your audience.

Some compliments work no matter who you're praising, as in telling someone how great they are looking today. But you won't compliment your child's teacher the same way you'll compliment your husband or your sister. For your compliments to resonate, try to key in on each person's individual motivations and personalities. For example, my son prides himself on acting mannerly, more so than my daughters, so I know that recognizing him for the times he has gone the extra mile of consideration rings especially true to him as a boost in acknowledgment. Yet at the same time, since he takes a laid-back approach to his appearance, I always compliment him when he's looking well put-together, to inspire him to follow this style more often.

CHAPTER FIVE

Four Essentials of the Most Effective Compliments

*Really big people are, above everything
else, courteous, considerate and generous
- not just to some people in some circumstances - but to everyone
all the time.*

~Thomas J. Watson, Sr.

*He who waits to do a great deal of good
at once, will never do anything.*

~Samuel Johnson

While I know you already have a basic understanding about how to compliment since you've given a few and gotten a few in return, I hope you're ready now for specific compliment advice—the juicy details of how to raise your own compliment quotient and make every compliment as meaningful and effective as possible.

Like any great recipe, we'll start with the basic ingredients that are mixed into the best compliments, remembering that, like grandmother's cherished recipes, this is not about being exact. It's more like a pinch of this and a scoop of that. Since compliments originate from and demonstrate the warmth of your heart, you don't have to worry about closely following some scripted procedures or restrictive formulas. You have a wealth of emotion and myriad opportunities to draw on for multiple different compliments. But with that said, successful compliments do rely on a few essential elements. Tap into this simple splendor and review these important ways to raise your compliment quotient.

ESSENTIAL ONE: Pay Attention

In order to offer a successful compliment,
you have to be an active observer.

The bottom line is you can't make compliments without paying attention! If you're busy juggling dinner and phone calls and helping with homework, you may miss something great to praise. With your partner or spouse, your children or colleagues, don't expect to interact with half your attention and find anything to compliment. You'll make compliments that are much more meaningful as you observe with a more discerning eye.

My friend Kimberly admitted to always being in a hurry at work and fixated on what her group has to get done. "Isn't everyone equally focused on getting through a meeting?" she says. But she decided to make an effort to stop and observe what had been accomplished—such as what it really took to get all the materials prepared, rather than simply assuming it was an easy task to complete—and make it a point to compliment on it. Her now-routine comments, "You all outdid yourselves getting all of this together and remembering to....." bring a positive vibration to the rest of the interaction. This builds the bones of a better relationship, just as taking your daily calcium supplements builds a stronger body.

Everything gets overlooked with familiarity and repetition, so for a compliment to be effective, you can't just say the same thing over and again. Of course you can recycle some compliments, but you need to keep looking and observing to stay in touch.

Reinforce your relationships with more observation.

ESSENTIAL TWO: Be Truthful

All compliments start with the seeds of truth.

A real compliment is always sincere, and there must be a grounding in honesty. When we think about speaking our truth, there seems to be a focus on the negative, as in, *we haven't been truthful before, but we're going to be truthful now, so watch out.*

But telling your truth can be accomplished through a compliment, as well. The question often used to demonstrate how tricky truth-telling can be is, "Honey, does this dress make my butt look big?" Numerous commercials and comedians have turned this scenario into a humorous nightmare of a confrontation between husband and wife.

But a truthful, "You are beautiful inside and out," or "Honey, you are always so beautiful to me," is not only a constructive response, it goes deeper, to the heart of their real, unspoken question, which is, "Even though I don't look exactly like I did when you married me, do you still think I'm beautiful?" or "Will you still think I'm beautiful when gravity has taken a bigger toll on me, as I think it has already?" The truth is, every situation has a positive and negative side. Your goal is to find the positive truths and handle the negative ones with a proactive strategy, such as redefining expectations, doing regular relationship tune-ups or counseling, perhaps.

You don't need a lot of material to give an honest compliment. And you don't have to wait for a perfect person or situation. Actually, compliments shine brighter in imperfect situations. But always remember that they shine brightest based on reality. Find a kernel of truth and start there. Even in glum situations, like surveying the results of your backed-up sewer line with the plumber, you can find a truth worthy of a compliment. In this case, this beleaguered worker will be happy to hear that you appreciate how they were on time or are working so quickly.

Don't worry about whether or not the other person believes your truthfulness. If you made the compliment out of a sincere place (and if it fits the situation), the receiver has the issue if he doubts your intention or insists you must want something for saying it.

If you have a sliver of a doubt about your intention in complimenting, do a quick internal motive check on it first. If it passes (and you'll know when that's true), then say it. Part of the truthfulness is not what you're saying, but being true to who you are, being an authentic you. Each and every one of your compliments may not be original or monumental, but if they are true for you, they will sound as if they are coming from your authentic voice.

If the authentic you has been a bit too shy to reach out with compliments to others, expand your compliment quotient slowly. Think of it as creating a ripple in the water, starting with more compliments to your inner circle of friends and relations and advancing outward with practice. As long as it's your voice and your values, you will make a sincere start.

Don't wait for perfect, as truthfully, we're all works in progress.

ESSENTIAL THREE: Get Specific

Customized compliments resonate more meaningfully

Sometimes you don't know someone well enough to give highly personalized praise. Yet giving all generic compliments begins to ring a bit hollow and raises suspicions about their genuineness. For instance, if you could "scratch and replace" what you're complimenting regularly in your spouse, child or friend with another person's name or deed, then you should consider expanding the range of your compliments and increase their impact.

"You look good," is not a bad thing for anyone to hear, of course. And some of us couldn't hear this enough. But it is less memorable or meaningful than, "That outfit really brings out the brilliant green in your eyes." After hearing that type of compliment, you'd remember to wear that green top the next time you have an important meeting, wouldn't you?

One evening my girlfriends were already standing in front of the restaurant where I was joining them for dinner, when Pat turned and exclaimed, "Look at you in those jazzy little boots!" as I walked up. I resisted the urge to tell her: that they were on sale at the end of the season last year; that I usually don't dress up like this all the time; that I wasn't sure if they looked good with the outfit. Instead, I felt an immediate boost. I gave her a big hug and said back, "Why thank you! They are cute, aren't they?" She had hit upon my secret pride of looking like a million bucks on a miserly budget. The fact that Pat was so specific with her compliment gave me that jolt of positive energy.

Of course, I wasn't merely repaying her compliment later when I commented on the fabric and fit of her cute red jacket. Instead, I simply flowed some of the loving energy back, also knowing that it was the type of apparel she likes to shop for and wear. In my compliment, I conveyed that she not only looked great but had made a great purchase decision, too.

Her pleased reaction reinforced to me the importance of getting specific in your compliments. The more precise you make your praise, the more meaningful it is to the receiver. When it rings more true inside them, the compliment produces a higher vibrational effect and yields more positive feelings.

Your more targeted compliments yield a bigger energy lift.

A Lesson On Being Specific From A Master Comedian

Oddly enough, one of the best—and most humorous—examples I've encountered of getting more specific in what you tell a person about himself comes in the form of a litany of insults. In the movie *Roxanne*, comedian Steve Martin plays a small-town fire chief with a very, very large nose, in a modern rendition of the story of *Cyrano de Bergerac*.

In a scene where a bully has insulted him by calling him "Big Nose" in a crowded bar, fire chief C.D. Bales tells the oaf that he should insult more eloquently if he's really going to bring it. Bales brags in front of the other patrons that he will come up with "better" insults, as many as the number the bully throws on a dartboard, which turns out to be 20.

May you be inspired in your compliments by these clever "better" insults—and have a chuckle or two. (Be aware, there are a few racy examples in here, too).

C.D. Bales: "Let's start with... Obvious: ''Scuse me, is that your nose or did a bus park on your face?'

"Meteorological: 'Everybody take cover, she's going to blow!'

"Fashionable: 'You know, you could de-emphasize your nose if you wore something larger, like... Wyoming.'

"Personal: 'Well, here we are, just the three of us.'

"Punctual: 'All right, Delbman, your nose was on time but YOU were fifteen minutes late!'

"Envious: 'Ooooh, I wish I were you! Gosh, to be able to smell your own ear!'

"Naughty: 'Uh, pardon me, sir, some of the ladies have asked if you wouldn't mind putting that thing away.'

"Philosophical: 'You know, it's not the size of a nose that's important, it's what's IN IT that matters.'

"Humorous: 'Laugh and the world laughs with you. Sneeze, and it's goodbye, Seattle!'

"Commercial: 'Hi, I'm Earl Scheib, and I can paint that nose for $39.95!'

"Polite: 'Uh, would you mind not bobbing your head? The, uh, orchestra keeps changing tempo.'

"Melodic: 'Everybody. He's got...' Everyone: [singing] 'The whole world in his nose!'

"Sympathetic: 'Aw, what happened? Did your parents lose a bet with God?'

"Complimentary: 'You must love the little birdies to give them this to perch on.'

"Scientific: 'Say, does that thing there influence the tides?'

"Obscure: 'Whoa! I'd hate to see the grindstone. Well, think about it.'

"Inquiring: 'When you stop to smell the flowers, are they afraid?'

"French: 'Saihr, ze pigs have refused to find any more truffles until you leave!'

"Pornographic: 'Finally, a man who can satisfy two women at once!'"

(Bales stops here to see how many more insults he has to go) "How many is that?," he says.

"Fourteen, Chief."

(He continues...)

"Religious: 'The Lord giveth... and He just kept on giving, didn't He?'

"Disgusting: 'Say, who mows your nose hair?'

"Paranoid: 'Keep that guy away from my cocaine!'

"Aromatic: 'It must wonderful to wake up in the morning and smell the coffee... in Brazil.'

"Appreciative: 'Oooh, how original! Most people just have their teeth capped.'"

[He pauses, pretending to be stumped, while the crowd urges him on...]

"All right.

"Dirty: 'Your name wouldn't be Dick, would it?'"

(Roxanne, 1987, Columbia Pictures Industries, IndieProd Company Productions, L.A. Films)

ESSENTIAL FOUR: Expand Your Vocabulary

*Abandon overused words for
more effective compliments.*

Adding colorful, descriptive, and unexpected words to your compliment vocabulary creates the most meaningful compliments. Powerful compliments happen through powerful words! Words that are overused or commonplace have a much less positive, vibrational effect. Of course, a platitude might be better than no compliment at all. But as advertising guru Claude Hopkins said, "Platitudes and generalities roll off human understanding like water on a duck's back."

Part of what you are trying to do with your compliment is make an impression. And to make the best impression, you have to gain another's interest and attention,. Improving your compliment quotient depends in part on your willingness, then, to increase the flavor in your compliments so they are savored even more. I'm talking about discarding bland, tired, overused and cliché phrases for more expressive word choices. (In case your old school-based antenna just started to hum, you're right; we're talking vocabulary here!) Don't abandon the quick and effective compliment standbys completely.

But trite words simply don't motivate like more bounteous, robust word choices.

Gather the Right Tools

Like Dad always said, "When all else fails, follow the directions," meaning, don't just wing it—get some help! Enhance your language and complimenting finesse by using these vocabulary resources for a few minutes a day—or a solid week or month. You decide what best fits your schedule:

Dictionary: A basic, of course. You don't need 18 volumes of the Oxford English Dictionary to get word-choice assistance. Have several different-sized dictionaries to stash around the house in different rooms. I shelve one in with the cookbooks, too, for quick reference in the kitchen. My kids also use www.dictionary.com regularly. Be careful about free downloadable software of course, in this age of computer viruses.

Thesaurus: Use the one that came with your word processing software, or any other online choice, and don't pass up a good old hand-held book. I get a special creativity bump just flipping the pages of a thesaurus, jumping around from word to word, a practice that seems to always stimulates further good ideas.

Magazines: If a child in the neighborhood sells subscriptions for their school, donate to the cause and get a copy of Reader's Digest and enjoy its monthly vocab section. You'll be surprised what you and your kids can learn if you do the quizzes with them. Practice using the words around each other.

Websites: Vocabulary.com is a staunch winner. And if you love sneaking education in with fun (and we need some fun, too, right?), check out www.freerice.com. For every correct definition of a word, the website donates 10 grains of rice through the World Food Programme. The levels get harder as you go. Vocabahead.com comes highly recommended from Gerry, a professional editor and writer, who says, it's fun, too.

Books: Your library may have a list of the vocabulary-building books it has on its shelves (perhaps for high schoolers to use when they're studying for the college entrance tests). Or, search for books on one of the many book websites. Nothing beats a trip to your local bookstore, of course. Find vocabulary-building books in the business or educational section. *Flocabulary: The Hip-Hop Approach to SAT-Level Vocabulary Building or Vocabulary Cartoons* are fun choices!

[Be sure to check out my website, www.complimentquotient. com, for more resources. In addition, two home-study courses will be available: ***The Busy Woman's Six-Week Guide to More Romance, More Connection, More Joy***; And a one-week e-class, ***Uplevel Your Language for Success: 7-Hour eCourse***]

I'm not talking about using different words just for the sake of using them. The effect of less-common words is actually science-based. Adding in unexpected words activates a part of the receiving person's brain into "alert Beta mode." And that is when you really reach them.

There are exceptions, of course, as I've said, most women would love to hear, "You look beautiful!" day after day and wouldn't get tired of it. But to really stimulate emotions, you have to get out of Alpha or sleep mode and into Beta mode. For instance, you're in Alpha mode when you get into your car and the next thing you know you're at work. Obviously you drove, but nothing made an impression, nothing particularly caught your attention. You can complete many habitual actions in Alpha mode, like putting on makeup, walking your dog, loading the dishwasher. But if, on your drive to work, you see emergency lights ahead, your attention has been heightened into Beta mode, a more active and alert phase. You slow down and pay closer attention as you try to merge past an accident.

Similarly, people tune out platitudes after a while. You want to cut through the regular clutter and engage the other's brain to make the most positive impact. "You're pretty" or "Good job" can be improved with better word choices, for example, "You're looking vivacious today" or "You are getting more adept at handling customer complaints."

With lackluster or half-hearted compliments, the gesture is only mildly effective, both in the vibrational effect on yourself and on others. The compliment giver and receiver activate their Beta states with a more vivid compliment exchange. The "reticular activator" has said to the brain, *"Hey, wake up out of Alpha, something great and exciting has just happened!"*

Not only that, but now that the brain has been jump-started, you are going to be searching around for other things to compliment. ("Wow, there are a lot of people wearing the luscious peach color today!") Or, the receiver will be inspired to pass along compliments as *they* begin to notice the vivaciousness of others around them. In this way, you can start a veritable avalanche of Beta-state, audacious compliments!

COMPLIMENTOLOGY TIPS

Exercise: Stop, look and listen.

Over the course of a day, stop to observe and list on paper ten remarkable traits about your (spouse, partner, child, mother, co-worker) that you haven't thought about in a while. Schedule about ten minutes the following day or two to talk to them and report on all the outstanding qualities and actions that you observed, or that you remembered by observing them closely again. Don't let them interrupt or try to negate what you are saying. Ask them to listen and soak in your compliments.

Ramp up from your point of view.

If you are uncomfortable using more lavish compliments about someone else (as in saying, "You look ravishing today"), focus on how the person's great qualities affect *you*. For example, you could get more descriptive by saying, "When you listen to me like this when we talk, I feel like the great communicator I have always known I could be." Or, "When you look me in the eye like that, I feel lavished on like a movie star. I love it!" This adds an element of authenticity that could appear to be lacking if you try to pour uncommon praise on another.

Never let vocabulary concerns stop you.

If words and language aren't your strong suit, throw out all the Essentials I reviewed regarding using more succulent and specific words and stick to what works for you! A simple, "You look great!" accompanied by a smile and a hug, still counts. And maybe as you experience the boost you get from releasing "the love hormone," oxytocin, from your hugs, you might be inspired to try to add some more amped-up words for your compliments.

Exercises: Plump up your compliments.

Practice finding more sumptuous words:

1. Use a thesaurus and find up with 5 synonyms/alternate phrases for *each* of these common words:

    Good:

    Nice:

    Pretty:

Keep the list handy to consult or memorize a few of these alternates to use in your next compliments.

2. Use more specific words when complimenting your children. Remain age appropriate, but try using more engaging words, as in "your fastidious way of doing your homework is sure to pay off in a better grade." (Words can be a great way to teach better vocabulary. If your children don't understand what you're saying, suggest they look up the unfamiliar words.)

RELATIONSHIPS AND YOUR COMPLIMENT QUOTIENT

CHAPTER SIX

Amplify Your Positive, Powerful Purpose with a Compliment Practice

Too often we underestimate the power of a touch, a smile, a kind word, a listening ear, an honest accomplishment, or the smallest act of caring, all of which have the potential to turn a life around.

~Leo Buscaglia

You can't live a perfect day without doing something for someone who will never be able to repay you.

~John Wooden

hrough the years, when it came to my routine of putting others' needs ahead of mine and trying to be and do it all, I often felt as if I were in the circus. While it may have occasionally felt like I was dealing with a clown or two, this circus feeling came by way of an act you may remember in which the performer tries to keep multiple plates spinning precariously high off the ground all at the same time. He starts a plate spinning on top of a thin stick, and then starts another plate on another stick, then another and another. Then he wildly runs from one plate to another, giving them each a bit more spin to keep them turning up on those sticks.

Running from home to work to school to home to functions to work to chores is a lot like spinning those plates, in hopes of keeping everything from crashing down. While we're hopping around the circus ring, we're draining ourselves more than we realize. And when we find ourselves empty, it's very difficult—some say impossible—to give to others. Sure, we do what we need to get done because we have to—but not joyfully. Or perhaps, as time goes on, less and less joyfully.

Some years ago I heard life coach and author Cheryl Richardson on *The Oprah Winfrey Show* talking about the techniques she used working with people as part of her *Life Makeover* process. She noted that most people have more trouble taking better care of themselves than doing anything else in her programs and that self-care is often seen as self-indulgent rather than the true filling-the-tank that it is. In the chapter, *"Finding Your Lost Self,"* she expands on that idea, noting, "Your relationship to yourself is at the heart of a great career, loving relationships, true joy and a meaningful life."

For those of us struggling to get out of the "others first" mode, giving more regular compliments works wonders as a pick-me-up because, by complimenting someone else, we get something back for ourselves—an indirect, vibrational benefit. By giving generously of our time, attention, and interest through more focused, more juicy, more unexpected compliments in all our relationships—romantic, family, friends, casual acquaintances—we can, surprisingly enough, be kinder to ourselves, filling our tanks and blossoming our joy.

Let's get to specific ways to raise your compliment quotient in five of our important relationship categories.

CHAPTER SEVEN

Relationship: Yourself

Build Your Own Bliss with Compliments

To love oneself is the beginning of a life-long romance.

~Oscar Wilde

One of the sanest, surest, and most generous joys of life comes from being happy over the good fortune of others.

~Robert A. Heinlein

We are each responsible for the state of our own spirits. Whether you see this as an opportunity or a problem, the truth as often repeated is that no one can make you happy or unhappy—it's an "inside job." One of the hardest lessons I have had to learn is that what's missing in any relationship is not just something the other person is failing to provide, not giving to me—it's also what I'm not giving to the relationship. And we can't expect others to give us what we don't give ourselves—why should they?

If you feel underappreciated by those around you, don't wait for others to recognize your efforts. Start on you, all by yourself. One easy and effective way to show your gratitude and enjoyment of your talents, your achievements, your life, even your body, is to give yourself compliments. Rhonda Britten, in her book, *Fearless Living™*, lists compliments as one of "One Hundred Proactive and Self-Affirming Behaviors," she recommends to get on what she calls your "Wheel of Freedom."

If you're not already in a habit of giving yourself "props," try giving yourself compliments such as these, that serve both as recognition of your wonderful self and essential wholeness *and* amp up your personal mojo in times when you are in need of inspiration.

"Girl, you cooked an excellent meal, in no time!"

"I am beautiful inside and out."

*"Of course I can finish this job; I'm patient, deter-
mined and talented."*

When I am in the midst of difficult writing assign-
ments I put one of my infamous sticky notes that say, "You
are a good writer!" on the side of my computer screen.
Seeing this compliment reminds me to smile, take a deep
breath and keep going, particularly when self-doubt or
procrastination threatens.

Giving compliments to others is also a highly effective addition to your self-care practices. Sharing a compliment with an acquaintance, friend or loved one brings on
a joyful jolt of energy, proven by scientific study. The *psy-
choneuroimmunology field* has confirmed that we experience an endorphin release when we turn up the edges of
our mouths and crinkle our cheeks and eyes—or, in simple terms, when we smile. When complimenting, we often
give our comment with a smile, receive a return smile
and then smile back again. So when you give a compliment to another, you both get a non-pharmaceutical boost
of spirits! Begin to increase the praise you offer on a daily
basis and you'll have a reliable way to shed the malaise
of a full-blown negative situation—or just a bad hair day.

Recently the flight I was catching at the airport was
delayed—and then delayed again. Then the monitors
throughout the terminal flashed that the flight was board-
ing, which had people running down the concourse, only
to find that, no, the plane wasn't actually leaving at that
time. And yet the gate agent got testy with these folks
who, one after another, breathlessly approached wondering what was going on. There was nothing to do except to
wait it out and get on board when we finally could.

At that time, I noticed a smartly dressed woman
standing ahead of me. After offering a quick compliment

to her about how youthful she looked in her sweater and matching earrings, I was able to pass the time pleasantly chatting with her, rather than descending into the mass frustration of the other passengers around us. The compliment gave us a boost of well-being amid the late-day disquiet and helped us salvage our peace of mind in spite of the situation.

Since women are such profoundly social creatures, the interaction that a compliment stirs up is good for us. The positive effect of my airport compliment-encounter has specifically been termed "social rest," according to Dr. Matthew Edlund, author of *The Power of Rest Why Sleep Alone is Not Enough*. This "interactive relaxation" we often think of as simply pleasant catch-up time with a friend has been determined to be as important as sleep in keeping us healthy and happy. So consider your friendly compliment interactions as filling a prescription for increased longevity and satisfaction.

Alter a dull, routine of a day by looking around for something to compliment in someone else. The compliment has the ability to profoundly change your energy level and your demeanor, even around a cranky co-worker or grumpy kid, because you are giving without expecting anything back. At these times especially, a compliment is a very high-vibrational action of generosity that creates enormous feelings of pleasure and goodwill.

FOUR PERSONAL PLUSES TO COMPLIMENTS

Take advantage of these four key qualities when using compliments to lift your own spirits:

Immediacy. One of the qualities of compliments I like best is that their effect registers not just today, but *this moment, right now*. Many experts speak to the spiritual and philosophical power of being in the moment, in understanding that the past is already written, the future is as yet an empty page. They note that how you elevate your experience of life, whether standing at the sink doing dishes or standing at the edge of a cliff watching a sunset, is by being in the present.

The win-win effect of a compliment is immediate. The "thank you!" or smile you receive back from the compliment you gave about, for example, someone's great-smelling perfume or the delicious salad they prepared, instantly uplifts both of you.

Don't give up the bigger contributions that make a difference in your sense of well being, of course, like donating time or money to a meaningful cause. Just remember that a quick, heartfelt compliment happens in the now and imparts its benefits immediately.

Practicality. Giving a compliment is inherently practical—and who doesn't like practical more than we multi-tasking types? Spread some cheer without running around and buying more stuff.

Like that Scout motto to "always be prepared," deciding to compliment more keeps you prepared with a simple gift for others that you can offer at any time, with no strings attached. Consider the person who always brings a house gift whenever she comes over. With her gesture, she can actually prompt negative feelings, as your desire to respond in kind can end up taking more time than you wanted to give to such a task. Instead of offering material goods, share a few specific, heartfelt compliments and enjoy your interaction in a less "consumable" way.

This is not only practical from a time standpoint, but it doesn't break the bank, and it raises the vibration around everyone involved—a sound investment if there ever was one.

Intimacy. In exchanging a compliment, the giver opens a window into her head and heart, exposing a bit of herself to the person who receives it. The moment when the compliment is received represents an intimate connection. In this way, giving a compliment creates a highly personal experience and imparts the benefits of deeper connection to our shared humanity.

Sometimes the person giving the compliment wades into personal territory she hadn't anticipated. For example, you might compliment a friend on a piece of jewelry, which you then find out was a gift from a special person or because of a particularly memorable event. If the event was a tragic one, this could be an awkward moment perhaps, but it is still an instant that bridges souls. In a world where many of us live on our own or away from extended family or loved ones, often feeling anonymous and lonely, these simple generous statements forge building blocks of friendship, community and love.

Multiplier. When you give a compliment, you get to reap what you sow. We have experienced how a compliment enhances the emotion of the person we're praising. But the jolt of delight you get in finding something to compliment, actually giving the compliment and witnessing the pleasure with which it's received, is a return gift to you and will carry over into other aspects of your life. A positive compliment breeds more positive emotions, thoughts, and experiences. Rinse and repeat.

Complimentology Tips

Exercise: Spirits-boosting game.

Your relationships flourish when you do. To fill your own emotional tank by increasing the number of compliments you're giving, play this simple game: Target a certain relationship group, for example: family; friends; those you don't know. Aim to give out x-number of compliments a day to people in one of these groups, perhaps even one a day or up to five or ten. Many of the people you compliment will respond with a "thank you," which is a great way to feel appreciated and more joyful. So keep score of how many of those *thanks* you receive in a day or a week—on paper, a note on your phone, a hash mark on your hand—whatever works for you. Look over your tally at the end of the day and re-live the emotional boost you felt from each expression of gratitude to you. Really soak all the good vibes you got. Let it buoy your spirits.

For example, I'll make it into a game when I'm trying to turn around my attitude and quit focusing on the negative. In this version, I often enter a store and aim to find one person to compliment before I leave. I might say something simple like, "cute purse" as I pass someone on an aisle or "that color looks good on you." The gestures often elicit a slightly surprised "thanks" from the recipients, which I "record" internally with some mutual delight.

If playing a game seems a bit flippant, think of it as a scientific experiment. Gather your compliment materials, take the necessary steps and record the results!

Muzzle the complaints.

You know when you are complaining too much. Or maybe you think you only criticize certain people or at certain times and think that's okay. Refocus your lens and strive to find something to praise instead.

Things you consider out of your control are often the easiest to complain about, such as the behavior of your co-worker, your child or your spouse. Yet often that's an excuse to avoid looking inward and seeing what is wrong with your life that you can control. Do some soul-searching, but be kind to yourself, as well. Compliment yourself, too, so that you feel worthy of a better work environment, a more helpful spouse or a less argumentative child. If you can do this, then you are on the road to attracting those things to you.

Expect compliments to lift your spirits.

If you're bored, or frustrated, or feeling down, find someone, even passing you on the sidewalk, and compliment your way into a better mood by expecting this practice to have a positive effect on you. When you expect something good to happen, you spark momentum in that direction, and life responds to your outlook. If you put that desire into recognizing and praising others, you cannot help but attract good back to you.

CHAPTER EIGHT

Relationship: Your Spouse or Partner

Arouse Your Romance With a Compliment Mindset

*For it was not into my ear you whispered,
but into my heart. It was not my lips
you kissed, but my soul.*

~Judy Garland

*Some women pick men to marry—
and others pick them to pieces.*

~Mae West

o you remember that magical time when our brains were turned on by our mates as much as our bodies? Whatever he uttered was interesting. Whatever she liked was intriguing. Whatever he repeated over and again was endearing. Whatever she ruminated about was fascinating. That magic may have lasted past dating and through those early, often pre-K times (not pre-kindergarten, but pre-kids). But then we're together for a while, and the bloom falls off the rose.

What happened to those heart palpitations at the sound of his voice? Are you pointing out his weak spots more often than enjoying his sweet spots? Why is it that the person we are closest to, depend on the most and share the most with can be the one the most difficult to praise? Why do we get stuck in the notion that it is our job to be in charge of another adult's behavior?

We can't put the bloom back on the rose in exactly the way it was before, nor would we want to. Committed, deeply felt love changes us. But we can revive our use of something that served us so well in the beginning. We can enlist the power of that biggest sex organ we all have, our brains, to grow a passionate mindset between ourselves and our partners—increasing our opportunity to put the rest of those intimate body parts to use while enhancing and strengthening our marriage or relationship.

The secret to compliments and our love relationships is the way they stir up our emotions on the way to stirring up our loins (in a nod to the romance-novel lingo). When our mind is full of unresolved issues—simmering arguments, poor communication, seeming betrayals—it's hard to stoke up the emotional closeness that is a major ingredient of passionate connectedness for women, in particular. After all, there is a huge difference between simply going through the motions and *enjoying* going through the motions.

How can we build back the intimacy and fire when we've built walls between us? Or maybe we have a rock-solid relationship but the flames have died down and we crave a more sizzling connection. While we might be tempted to look to something outside us to boost our interest or amp up our connection, there is a better option.

Compliments may not be able to resolve more difficult trust issues, outside stressors, too much alcohol or zero couple-alone time because of too much parenting time. And when you are extremely upset (ticked off, I think, is the word), it's admittedly harder to switch on the peaceful, positive feelings toward your partner. But just a tiny encouraging thought or phrase provides you with a jump-start in the right direction. Your compliments can be a bit-by-little-bit means to stimulate a loving, accepting, and intimate atmosphere from which to grow your passionate connection again.

Think about when you're feeling impatient, overwhelmed or frustrated with your mate. You are likely to forget that none of these states actually have anything to do with him. You are allowing yourself to think he is causing this experience when, actually, you are creating it yourself, as your reactive emotions are completely under your control. (Again, what seems to be part of the problem is actually an opportunity.) You are giving your power away in the situation when you stay in the place of blame or resentment.

As we have discussed, compliments have an action, an immediacy, a way of taking control of what feels out of control and creating a new intention. Compliments allow you to build an emotional connection that's lost, missing, hidden away, forgotten. They allow you to focus on what's right, not what's *not* working, what didn't get done, what you have to do later. It brings you smack into the now, into the love deep in your heart, which then opens you up to all forms of joy.

In order to give a compliment, we have to recognize the good (at least one praiseworthy thing) and forget (at least for the moment) the bad. That's right, we have to refocus on something we can recognize with a compliment, which then kick-starts our emotional connections. By letting the not-so-right flow through us and away, we open up the opportunity to fill that now vacant place with something that sparks our hearts.

One way to get started is to lead by example. Build lighthearted intimacy through loving, even playful compliments. Start by telling him how he makes you feel so sensual when he looks at you *that way* or other personalized compliments about how you feel about him—his looks, his touch, his thoughtfulness, his skills at making coffee ...or making love. Don't overlook smaller recognitions, as well. Flattering your romantic partner about how great he looks in those jeans today, or how good his pancakes were, can go a long way to shoring up your loving relationship.

Remember when you always tried to look your best for each other? Before "kid clothes," I suspect. No, not the clothes the kids are wearing but the clothes we busy moms choose to wear—wash and wear, to be exact. With a bit of complimentary flirting you unleash that brain-banked emotional memory of the time you dressed well for each other. You revive romance and connection and who knows what other kinds of put-off endeavors. And with a romantic partner, there are virtually no worries about crossing lines with flattery, as we have discussed previously.

Men need to hear compliments as often as women. Praising what he remembers to do for you is a hundred times more effective than pointing out what he forgot. Make him feel special and appreciated by complimenting on anything you can think of—from the effort he put into deciding to shave for the evening to how he fixed the remote to how great he is at telling a joke.

Don't forget that you can give praise using something as simple as sweet-talk. Sweet-talk is heart-based. You don't need a degree in it, you just need to let your love flow. Sweet-talk is a breath of fresh air after a dusty long day. It is affectionately romantic. Sweet-talk reminds your partner that you think the sun rises and sets with them, at least for the moment. "You are so smart!" "You are totally good-looking!" "You are a terrific kisser!"

I know that when there is tension already between the two of you, this may be the hardest of all times to compliment. But dig deep into the "give what you want to get" inner core. If you've been on a downward communication spiral or even swept up in kid-commitments and dull routines, compliments can lift everyone's spirits and give your relationship the small boost it needs to start an upward spiral. As I heard the author of *1001 Ways to Be Romantic*, Greg Godek, say, perhaps what most couples really need in order to rekindle their relationship is simply more romance. He called it "radical romance," not meaning some form of romance that might be difficult to enact or gone to extreme heights. He meant radical in its frequency—active, on-going, regular, amorous attention rather than something saved for a special occasion, like an anniversary or occasional night out.

Of course, your spouse may not understand that your compliments are meant to encourage him to compliment you in return as a way to spark your desire. After all, many men need only think about their partners wanting to meet them in the bedroom to be ready for a passionate encounter. We need to let our partners know that we could use some help pushing some of the brain-fog out of our minds before sex, and compliments are a great place to start.

Share with him how every woman wants to hear how much her partner enjoys seeing her, exactly as she is. Explain that this is where desire starts—that when you feel beautiful, it's easier to feel comfortable with your body in every way; that when he shares his appreciation of you, you're much more willing to shed those pounds of things-to-do in your brain, and perhaps some layers of clothing along the way. Tell him that nothing makes you feel more beautiful than hearing that no matter what you think of your thighs or your arms or your neck, he sees you as hot and gorgeous. I've been reassured that men aren't looking at our bodies the way we do—with all our thoughts about our flawed body parts—but seeing us as the sum of a woman, a warm, luscious female, with all the ingredients they cherish and enjoy. Let his compliments about your body boost your feelings about your physicality and, in turn, your desire to get physical more often. If he is still not forthcoming on the compliments, begin a hearty conversation with yourself to ramp up your own mojo.

Way to go thighs, getting me up all those stairs!

I love my luscious lips!

I am a great cook and know how to get cookin'!

As I share elsewhere in the book, we are biologically primed to find favor with those who are interested in us, so you have an automatic advantage for influencing your relationship with your spouse or partner. Spark more romance and desire by building the habit of seeing and stating the good in your marriage instead of the bad to cross over the distance created by small irritabilities, being taken for granted and the little criticisms we think are our job to deliver. Be more of the loving presence you desire.

Click Off The Gulf Between The Sexes

I often take 15-minute "vacations" at the grocery store. Not, perhaps as some of you might think, shopping by myself and enjoying the pleasure of not having to negotiate everything that goes into the cart. I'll take a few minutes to browse in the greeting card aisle.

While there, I often peruse the funnier cards to get a few chuckles. (Pathetic-sounding, I know, but sometimes I laugh so loud, I wonder if they're going to call security!) One recent humorous birthday card I stumbled upon (from DCI Studios, Tomato Cards) cleverly highlighted the man-woman divide. The front depicted **"The Woman's Remote"**, with the inside reading, *On your birthday—may you get exactly what you've been wishing for!* The imaginary remote control device featured, among others buttons: **OFF** the couch. **SET** the table. ♠ **Thermostat.** ♥ **Toilet seat. MUTE** sports. **MUTE** snoring.

But the two sets of buttons that caught my attention on this supposed female joystick were: ⬆ **Romance**. ⬇ **Sex**. And: **STOP** Complaining. **START** Complimenting.

Laughter is great medicine, but this funny card planted the seeds of something serious—the suggestion that women might contemplate what they're giving and expecting in return.

We have to take responsibility for our half of a relationship. What did you do at the outset of the relationship that you're no longer doing? What are the things you focus on, the things that create the essence of the relationship's energy? Can you get past the-chicken-and-the-egg thoughts about who should start complimenting who and when? If the position of the toilet seat (or whatever you complain about) is a line in the sand between you two, maybe this "little thing" is indicating a much bigger problem and your relationship truly needs more help. In any case, consider what buttons would be on "The Man's Remote" and where you might find ways to up your compliment quotient together.

Complimentology Tips

Be a stranger.

Start giving more sincere compliments to your partner by stepping back and looking at him occasionally like a stranger would—a coworker, another parent at the ball field, a neighbor. What talents do these folks notice that you ignore? What does your guy do that you take for granted? By expressing your positive observations, you are reminding your partner of that part of him that recognizes his glorious self, the part that gets underappreciated in the impersonal world around him. Heighten your connection by reflecting his genius back to him.

Make a fuss.

If you worry about spoiling your guy, try putting the shoe on the other foot. How much would it spoil *you* to hear, "You look ravishing!" over and again? No, I didn't think you'd mind! Who else do you think is complimenting your partner? Not his pushy boss. Or your kids (unless they want his car for date night or to get the new X-box game!). Be the one who rekindles his flame and stokes his confidence. "You look so good to me, darling."

Focus on respect.

For some reason, we tend to think of respect as an outside job, not something you get from an insider such as your spouse. But men particularly appreciate being recognized for their achievements, especially by those *they* respect (which would be you—you had the good sense to pick him, after all; and if you're the mother of his children, what man doesn't respect that life-carrying force, even if they don't say so?). Think of how you feel when you are complimented on a job well done. Choose to be the person whose compliments make a difference in your partner's life.

Unearth your flirt.

Don't let embarrassment stop you from giving flirting another go. Flattery is the perfect romantic affection-builder. Extending the length of time you build up to lovemaking with flattery and flirting are brain-tapping ways to increase the passion. Re-vamp your foreplay to include some verbal connection.

In public and around the kids, try simple words of appreciation: "I appreciate you following up to call the exterminator like you promised." (As a friend of mine said, definitely flirting words!) Whispered, personalized, more romantic flirting—still simply talking—can further generate heat.

Remember: flirtatious compliments restore a bit of the luster in your relationship, rekindling the newness you both felt, before your life together became so habitual. Research has revealed that part of the excitement of a new relationship is just that, the newness. Nothing is wrong with safety and comfort and familiarity, of course. This is a large part of the meaningfulness of marriage and committed relationships. But when the everyday overtakes our relationships, it can become too easy to simply let the spark die. Flirtatious compliments are one spark that can re-create some of the newness that keeps a lifelong love affair simmering in your hearts.

Private—Members Only

Recently, I unearthed some lingo from MTV's infamously outrageous show Jersey Shore (no, not from watching the show but from an article I read about the show's unique phraseology). In Jersey Shore talk: Vibing = flirting. Smushing = making love. Spark desire by creating your own passionate code words. Men are often more adept at this than women, so give your partner some leeway to use words of all kinds. Not all romantic language has to be frilly; it can be sweet, spicy, sentimental, or sensual. Put your heads together and create your own secret romantic language filled with passionate compliments. Add in a heaping of body language and a helping of suggestion to really build up interest!!

Top 5 list.

Take a cue from *Late Show with David Letterman's* most popular segment, Top Ten lists, and create a compliment list to build more connection with your romantic partner. Set a deadline (tomorrow night, the weekend) for each of you to write down at least 5—or go for the full ten—compliments about the other. Make a point to share your lists, on the same night or you on one night, him on another. At the very least, you'll go to sleep with a smile of appreciation on your face!

Visit your memorable-moments vault.

One of the best ways to intensify lovemaking pleasure and, therefore, help increase your desire to experience it more often is said to be through extended foreplay, which doesn't only have to mean kissing and touching. Unleash powerful emotions to boost up your desire by recalling pleasurable memorable times and giving compliments about them:

The wonderful way he touched you when...

The amazing way he smelled when...

The sensual feel of his kisses when ...

How you felt when he told you how beautiful you look in that light...

How skilled he was focusing on your pleasure when....

Unleash your romantic heroine.

Nothing amps up your ability to flatter a partner like reading an occasional romance novel (remember flattery = verbal foreplay). If it's not your regular cup of tea, breeze through a few of these books at the library or pick some up at the used bookstore. They'll help you find some specific, fun, whatever level of x-rating language you're comfortable with to unleash on the "Fabio" in your life and jumpstart some more light-heartedly passionate intimacy.

CHAPTER NINE

Relationship: Your Family

Nourish Your Loved Ones With Compliments

There is an unfortunate disposition in man to attend much more to the faults of his companions that offend him, than to their perfections which please him.

~Greville

Growing up in a large family with five daughters and one son, I remember a life full of school, meal times, play times, household chores, kids' activities and special life events, such as graduations, weddings and the like—not particularly fancy or perfect, but I thrived in this family-carnival atmosphere (at its height, my mom called our house "Grand Central Station," in which she was the loving, busy train conductor) and always knew I wanted more than one child. I appreciated the swirl of activity and wanted my children to have siblings (though I have heard at one time or another they all wished they were the only child!).

But before I became pregnant with my second child, I began to worry about whether having another would be a good idea, because I loved my first child, a daughter, so completely, so totally—how could I have enough love for another helpless baby? Could I possibly bond with another child the same way?

The answer came in the form of a saying I enthusiastically embraced, especially since we went on to have a third child: *love is not a pie, it's an ocean.* As other longtime parents already knew, my second and third children didn't require me to divide my love; instead, they caused it to grow exponentially. I didn't have to worry about divvying it up, as love simply begot more of itself. It's easy to translate this to many other parts of life: success is not a pie; abundance is not a pie; luck is not a pie; friendship is not a pie, etc.

The generosity of compliments acts in the same way. You simply don't have to ration complimenting one child or sibling so that you have enough compliments left for another. You don't have to ration complimenting now, so that you have enough later, just in case someone does something else better another time. And the good feelings engendered through compliments grow more of the same.

Compliments can do all kinds of lifting in a family, as we already discussed in the chapter about the power of compliments, because they are gratitude, generosity, praise, respect and appreciation all rolled into one powerful practice. When so much resentment and anger fill up the spaces, it can seem difficult to opt for a compliment: don't you need to communicate how badly you feel or how bad the situation is in order to define it, to analyze it, to fix it? Simply put, no—not most of the time.

I always worried that I would encourage a landslide of bad behavior if I didn't point out—if I let slide—what my children did wrong. But all of our admonitions add up over time, so we have to be careful about what we say (though as we said, our actions speak even louder than what we say). Sure, their antics can seem deliberate and defiant. But by constantly building the picture of the bad behavior, we are continually attracting more of it. "You're a nuisance." "Don't be such a baby." "You're so awkward." When we deliver these negative statements—often in a highly emotional moment—we only emphasize the defects, and because our words are wrapped in the power of emotion, we cause a greater likelihood that those will be remembered. People, especially our children, consciously and subconsciously grow into our vision of them. By constantly criticizing your children, we change the way they see themselves, and not for the better.

Susan Jeffers, in her book *Feel the Fear and Do It Anyway*™, explains how we can encourage the opposite: "[I]n some strange way," she writes, "when we praise the people in our lives, we release the negativity and open the door for their being loving toward us."

That's part of the funny thing about it: we want others to overlook at least some of our faults and love us anyway. We want others to simply forget the times we dropped the ball, got angry over something little, or "freaked out," as the kids say. We want those around us to support us as we try to learn new things and new behaviors. So we must be those same supportive people for others.

Instead of focusing on the bad habits of others, it's important to remember that regular praise for something well done provides the fuel to power the creation of good behavior or habits. By congratulating your children, you provide recognition of their achievements and help build their sense of esteem. Praising them for their good ideas has the same effect, whether or not you actually put those ideas to use.

Some parenting articles note that we should praise our kids not for an outcome (a grade they achieved) but for the process (they studied hard). These articles argue that only praising the result puts the focus on the outcome, encouraging achievement at all costs.

But my friend Jeannie, for one, would disagree. Jeannie went through her childhood constantly hearing from her father how unintelligent and incapable she was, even though she regularly brought home solid grades while helping take care of her siblings. Until you are already giving more praise than criticism to those in your life, I'm not sure hair-splitting about praising the outcome rather than the process is worth stopping you from praising more often.

Neither would I suggest worrying too much about hurting another's child's feelings when you praise a sibling. Of course, kids are the first to tell you "that's not fair" if they perceive something out of balance in your treatment of them in relation to your other children. But when you compliment a sibling, this shows all of your children that they can earn their own praise, too. And in this way, you can train them to be generous not just with their actions but also with their words. You can put the brakes on denigrating and belittling conversation by being the one on whom they model their behavior.

50 Ways to Praise A Child

Often sent home from school or as a gift from an insurance agent, like I once got, if you need some compliment inspiration, paste this list on your refrigerator:

Wow - Way to go - Super - You're special - Outstanding - Excellent - Great - Good - Neat - Well done - Remarkable - I knew you could do it - I'm proud of you - Fantastic - Super star - Nice work - Looking good - You're on top of it - Beautiful - Now you're flying - You're catching on - Now you've got it - You're incredible - Bravo - You're fantastic - Hooray for you - You're on target - You're on your way - How nice - How smart - Good job - That's incredible - Hot dog - Dynamite - You're beautiful - You're unique - Nothing can stop you now - Good for you - I like you - You're a winner - Remarkable job - Beautiful work - Spectacular - You're spectacular - You're darling - You're precious - Great discovery - You've discovered the secret - You figured it out - Fantastic job

(From the Illinois Department of Children & Family Services (DCFS) website, http://www.state.il.us/dcfs/images/praiseAChild.html.)

Respectful, courteous kids don't happen by chance. By freely handing out compliments, you can create a ripple that expands out from your immediate world.

The same is true across your family—for your siblings, parents, and other relations. Know that those in your family watch you. If you are lucky enough to have generous, loving parents and siblings, let them know it with regular, positive feedback. If you aren't that lucky, set your own good example and be gracious instead of gossipy as often as possible.

Complimentology Tips

Try some simple phrases.

I know that as you interact with your family throughout the day, you will find many ways to raise your compliment quotient. Here are a few ways you may or may not have already thought of to compliment your children:

"You must be proud of that." The most effective, affirming compliments work not by comparing someone to others, but by recognizing a person's inherent worth on their own. Keep telling your children: "I am really proud of you."

"You are so cute." "You look so pretty today." "You are so handsome!" No matter how we would prefer it to be, we live in a visual world that often judges and labels people based on their exterior appearance—hair, height, skin, features. While it might seem superficial in contrast to more substantial ways of growing your child's potential, it is perfectly natural and delightful to tell your kids they look good and inspire them to take care of them-

selves. You are not creating egotistical monsters (unless there are other negative forces at work) and, in fact, you are shoring up their self-esteem, which can help eliminate their need to engage in self-destructive activities to boost their egos.

"You did a good job!" Kids today are under more stress than we realize. I believe that the level of coursework my kids experience in high school is nearly on a par with the work I did in college in many respects. Add in all the other activities kids are enrolled in these days and the high expectations of their parents and teachers, and, yes, they are stressed. So listen to them talk about their activities and schoolwork without interrupting, and after they've expressed themselves, find ways to compliment them on what they deem important to have accomplished. It might be different than what you expect.

Exercise: Hone in with specifics.

During the next week, select one particular event or action your child (or another family member) did, such as finish his homework or help with a meal. Get out a sheet of paper or onto your computer and list at least five individual parts of that action or event on which you could comment positively. For example, instead of a quick and general "thanks for helping" when your child helps you make dinner, divide your compliment into specifics:

1) You responded so quickly when I asked for help—thank you.
2) You got out all the ingredients I asked for so efficiently. You really paid attention.

And so on.

Make a point to share the actual list or to give at least one specific instead of general compliment the next time they do the same thing.

Exercise: Create compliment memorabilia.

Add a special compliment element to bring family memories to life in future times.

1. Do you save your children's report cards and achievement papers? Write a compliment on them before you put them away. This way, when they pull them out a year, 5 years, 10 years later, the saved memorabilia will be even more meaningful.

2. Along the same lines, find a meaningful photo of you and your siblings, perhaps from when you were younger or just from a memorable time. Make a copy for everyone in the family and frame them. Send one off to each person with a note complimenting them on something—maybe about something you've never shared before from the past. Try sending it when it's not a regular holiday or birthday (unless you don't normally send presents at those times). It will make the gesture all the more special.

Model loving praise.

Remember that the best way to influence your children is by example, so compliment others in your children's presence. Studies reveal over and again that children of all ages are sponges, watching what we are doing and making subconscious mental notes to follow in our footsteps. The impression they take in by seeing what we as grownups do is much stronger than what they absorb by our quacking at them over and over. Let them hear you complimenting those you don't know to help develop their tolerance and appreciation of others as well as seeing examples of polite, generous actions out in the world.

CHAPTER TEN

Relationship: Your Friends

Add Compliments to Buoy Your Friendships

A friendship can weather most things and thrive in thin soil; but it needs a little mulch of letters and phone calls and small, silly presents every so often - just to save it from drying out completely.

~Pam Brown

omen rock. I could say we rule the world and only let men think they do, but I want to be careful not to imply male-bashing in any form. We need and love our husbands, fathers, sons, brothers, and boyfriends; I just have lots of out-and-out sisterhood-affection from years of wonderful relationships with women. I grew up with four sisters (and a great brother). I have lots of girl cousins whom I always adored as well as girlfriends whom I couldn't live without, from grade school and slumber parties all the way through college adventures. I have worked largely with women and mostly for women bosses, and I have volunteered as a Big Sister-mentor and in senior centers populated largely, yes, by elderly women. I'm not alone in my many female interactions. Today, women are enjoying renewed opportunities of camaraderie in many ways, from book groups and Bunco nights—which are really just our moms' and aunts' bridge and "coffee klatches" (with wine instead, right?) .

We need, want and can't live without our *sisters,* and compliments are vital parts of that "mulch" that Pam Brown says we need in order to sustain our friendships. Even the best of friendships and sibling relationships, the kind where you let your hair down; where you allow each other to be completely who you are; where you say what's honest and true; even these friendships need the watering of praise and hearty congratulations.

Consider, for example, my friend Andrea. A friend of hers comes to her rescue repeatedly, offering a ride to the auto-repair shop or watching her kids at the last minute, but rarely asking for help in return. Andrea's friend is a single mother, with children who probably aren't telling her very often how they value what she does for them or how pretty she is. So when Andrea wants to return some of the support her friend gives her in those concrete ways, she reaches out in another way—through compliments. Andrea nurtures their friendship by relating how thankful she is that her friend returns phone calls or email so quickly, reinforces how much she values her friend's take on current events and reminds her as often as appropriate how cute her haircut, yoga pants or shoes are. This doesn't cost anything but yields tremendous results for all.

Another friend of mine commented that perhaps women think other people are complimenting our friends, and so we tend to leave each other out of our compliments. In fact, one evening, after receiving a compliment on a certain coat I wear a lot, I thanked the person, noting that no one had ever commented on it before. The woman was genuinely surprised and said, "I almost didn't say anything because I figured you heard this all the time." Well, no, I hadn't.

Do you hold back because you think the other person always looks pulled together, so they must hear compliments all the time? Or worse, because you judge them undeserving of a compliment simply because their positive qualities appear to come natural to them? Maybe you think she's a great cook naturally, but perhaps in reality, it's a skill she's honed at the mercy of burned pots and pans and batteries for her smoke detector, and she would relish a little praise on the dish she shared. Or maybe you think she must hear often how good she looks; after all, she looks X-pounds thinner than you. But perhaps she had struggled to lose weight after giving birth and now stays in shape with a regular exercise program and would love to hear something about her appearance. Why do we seem to think everyone's lives are perfect—and therefore not deserving of compliments, while we allow ours to be messy and busy and imperfect—and therefore in need of support and commendation?

My friend Kristi always comes across as gorgeous and self-confident and "together." Sure, she's had some of the benefits some of the others of us don't, in her more afflu- ent lifestyle growing up and a happy home life now. But she relishes hearing a compliment, too, as much as any of us. Why wouldn't she?

Similarly, my friend Amy came from a challenging up- bringing, though now she has a great husband and two beautiful children, and lives in an area abundant with close, friendly neighbors. Amy consistently shows her generous nature with easy expressions of compliments and gratitude. Shouldn't she receive similar consider- ation from others?

Perhaps it's the truthful part of compliments that gets sticky for some friends. Truth is necessary to friendship, but brutal truth is not friendly. Certainly, your friends don't expect you to lie to them in an effort to compliment you. Yet you can always focus on the good to find some- thing true to commend to your friend. And if there is something less positive you also wish to convey, you can lessen the blow by starting with the truthful compliment before being more forthcoming about the less flattering sort of comment for which friends rely on each other. Re- cently on *The View* television show, both Whoopi Gold- berg and Barbara Walters stated that they would start out a conversation where they were concerned about a friend's weight (gain or loss) by commenting on how good they look now, but bringing up their concern for their future health.

After buoying each other, after being there for each other, after sharing soul-touching moments, a generous compliment is one of the greatest gifts we can give to our friends. On a cold day of disappointment or a time when a friend is feeling overwhelmed, offering a compliment is sharing a bit of sunshine. You help them re-write a bad story of a day by sparking their recognition of their inner genius—and goddess—rather than their memory.

This is neither shallow-minded nor inconsequential to your friends' wellbeing. In reflecting back to them their grandest selves, they remember why they are here, and together you create more joyfulness and wholeness around you.

Complimentology Tips

Jump in and compliment often.

Don't weigh and measure your compliments among your friends or acquaintances. If you are moved to say something, you can keep it short and sweet—it doesn't have to be a long, drawn out compliment. Give a quick, "You're glowing today!" and you may never know that that was the only nice thing that person heard all day.

Encourage good friend behavior.

Compliment your friends in your children's presence. When one of my daughters first got her braces, I told her they weren't that noticeable, that she still had a beautiful smile. But it was the text message she got from one of her girlfriends, Allison, that made all the difference. After texting to Allison that she had gotten her braces on, Allison instantly texted back: "I think u r pretty." That brought a smile to my daughter's face like my own words couldn't. Encourage your children to support their own friends in this generous way by modeling it in your everyday behavior.

Declare a no-whining zone.

Once in a while, declare a no-complaint zone when you get together with friends. Of course, having friends to whom you can tell everything is important, but every so often decide to ban all negative talk and simply focus on each other's good points. Exact a "fine" for each time someone violates the ban and use that money for the next non-negative (aren't two negatives a positive?!) night.

Start a new tradition.

Japan's unique Valentine's Day tradition (started in the 1950's) of women giving men a gift of *honmei choco* (sweetheart chocolates), has been declining in recent years. The practice of giving *tomo choco* (friendship chocolate) to female friends is growing instead. A recent survey in Japan indicated that 74 percent of women planned to give a Valentine's gift to a female friend, but only 32 percent intended to buy something for a boyfriend. And 92 percent of respondents said that they had gotten the chocolates from a friend last year.

News sources attribute this change to several potential causes. One is that the prevalence of texting, online and other digital forms of interaction make the exchange of tomo choco a perfect excuse to get together with busy girlfriends in person. The other is that friendship chocolates are usually a less expensive gift than the sweetheart chocolates, or the 10 to 30 boxes of *giri choco* (obligation chocolates) that women are supposed to give to all the men in their lives, including bosses, co-workers, brothers, etc.

Since we know that other women like chocolate as much as we do, why not follow Japan's lead? Consider having a girl's night out dedicated to praising each other for something others may have overlooked and bring each other a bon-bon treat, too. (The survey also indicated that older women are less likely to buy chocolates to confess their love. Perhaps they are using more compliments to their loved ones, instead!)

CHAPTER ELEVEN

Relationship: Others

Expand Your Positive Impact Around You

The deepest principle in human nature is the craving to be appreciated.

~William James

When you reach out, the chances are pretty good that someone will reach back.

~Cheryl Richardson

omplimenting those we don't know well—or at all—can have the most profound effect on our well-being. This may be the truest form of generosity, as we get nothing obvious in return—maybe a "thank you" or even a quick compliment back, but certainly expecting nothing more substantial than that.

When you compliment someone unknown to you, or someone you know only by sight or brief acquaintance, you are actually experiencing the vibrational, endorphin-producing "high" that comes with giving. Surveys that ask why volunteers donate their time reveal that, yes, the volunteers want to make a difference. But nearly all volunteers also talk about the good feeling they get when they donate to a cause and how this feeling is unlike any other they get by doing well in their jobs or doing right by their families. When it comes to compliments, this giving of yourself not only produces a high, but it also evokes feelings of belonging and camaraderie.

Of course, complimenting a stranger also works wonders on the recipients of your attention, as it fulfills part of your intention to be a loving presence in the world. You have no idea what someone else went through the minute before you encountered him or her, let alone the hours or days before. Maybe the person was having an enjoyable day and your compliment made the day even better. On the other hand, maybe the person has had a very trying day and your compliment was a much-needed boost.

You might be tempted to not say anything. Perhaps you don't feel particularly charming or outgoing at the moment. But that shouldn't stop you, say the experts. Evidence proves that the physiological impact of a making a smiling face can improve your mood on its own. Sharing a smile and a few positive words, even when you don't feel happy, will nourish your own spirits as well as those around you, at the same time.

Perhaps you are tempted to hold back a compliment because it seems as if you are making a commitment to this person. Keep in mind that nothing long-term need come into play. Common courtesy doesn't imply anything long-lasting, yet is extremely appreciated. And the reverse is true, too. Just because someone has complimented you doesn't mean you owe them anything in return.

If you are just starting out complimenting those you don't know very well, note that it's common to be a little nervous. All new endeavors mean some sort of change is taking place, and change can elicit fearful feelings.

But I'm Too Shy!

Those who get to know me are surprised to learn that I used to be shy, since now I talk easily to almost anyone, often to my children's chagrin if they are out with me. From a little girl hiding behind her parents, tucked in between their legs, I slowly grew out of my shyness sometime around high school and college, finally, to the benefit of my early adult life in various jobs, travelling, and on into my career and marriage. When I stepped back from the workforce to be home with my kids when they were young, my shyness re-emerged. It happened pretty quickly; I guess a few years of outings limited to the park, library and grocery store can do that to you, even if you have great mom-friends.

As I found myself once again trying to get un-shy I learned a few things. One is that there's nothing wrong with having a more nuanced approach to joining a conversation—first observing before deciding when to jump in. Second, that making conversation in general is a skill that can be learned and, as I had discovered, unlearned and relearned.

Like small talk, giving compliments, too, comes more naturally with practice. I compare it to the need to exercise to keep muscle tone as I age. If you don't flex your compliment muscle, you can lose it. Luckily, you can strengthen it, too. Similar to an exercise program that works your biceps, triceps and other muscles in the human body (though you don't need to consult your doctor before starting), you can start slowly and keep building your compliment strength.

Assuage your nervousness by focusing on the other person and the good you're about to share. If you're new to complimenting those outside your inner circle, start close to home, with a neighbor, your postal carrier, the librarian. If you're more practiced, look for opportunities to share a compliment with people you simply encounter along the way, shopping next to in the grocery store or someone you may see regularly by not talk to.

Concentrate on how *you* feel after you receive a compliment. Remember: when all else is difficult, return to love. As the saying goes, "Love wasn't put in your heart to stay; love isn't love 'til you give it away." The refrain may sound corny, but sharing a compliment with someone you happen to see or meet is a generous way of spreading love. And since the world is in desperate need of more constructive, affirmative interactions, this is one way you can do your small part.

Finally, just because you don't know the person well, don't skip the compliment essentials. Pay attention; be truthful in what you say; get specific. Don't make your compliment long and involved, aggressive or too imposing. Use a friendly tone and attitude, and smile! Once you raise your compliment quotient, you'll wonder how you got along any other way.

Complimentology Tips

Be curious.

Try to leave your snap judgment-reflex behind when talking with a stranger. Don't focus on what the person is wearing or some annoying habit they may have. Instead, ask about their life. As you converse and dig a little deeper into their circumstances, you might find a snippet of detail you can compliment. Perhaps the difficult colleague in the meeting with you has been dealing with a sick father. You can then compliment her on her devotion to him, instead of grumbling to yourself about something that might have irritated you about her before you began chatting.

Accept differences.

Face it—as much as we'd like to be able to have folks do things "our way," the world would be a very boring place if everyone did just that. Sure, you might not have picked out that purse, or you might think those shoes are highly impractical, But celebrating these choices with a compliment is not hypocritical, it is accepting. Complimenting someone's choice of something you don't like is not lying; it's merely showing non-judgmental respect for the ways in which we all differ. Of course, you shouldn't say, "I love that couch" if you don't; but you could comment that it really looks good in the room, that it looks like their style of furniture, or that it was great they got such a good deal on the couch and are happy with it.

Take small opportunities.

Acknowledging someone you know casually or have never met by quickly giving that person a compliment is simple and easy. Don't let the opportunity pass by because your kind thought doesn't seem "monumental" enough to mention. My friend, Allison, for example, particularly enjoys complimenting other women she encounters in her day-to-day doings. "The other day, I was passing by a woman in a bright pink raincoat waiting for a bus and I told her what a great color it was," she said. Allison commented that with all of the tan and black raincoats she had seen already that day, the pink one really stood out, and she felt like she simply had to tell this woman that she looked great in it. Allison doesn't worry that such a compliment is too trivial to mention; she not only enjoys the lift she gives others but the boost she gets herself from doing this.

Be present.

Standing in line at the grocery store, it's easy to focus on how your future agenda is on hold: the checker is gabbing more than checking; the customer is taking so much time to pay; the clerk is oh-so-exactly putting things into sacks. By switching the tone of the experience through appreciation in the now, you can shift the vibration of the interaction for everyone.

For example, I might tell the customer ahead of me that his child is so well behaved sitting in the grocery cart during checkout. Or I might compliment the clerk on her wedding ring. (A woman has either worn her ring so long she's almost forgotten about its beauty, or it's new enough that she's thrilled someone else noticed. People instantly run through a video in their mind of shopping for the ring, receiving it on their wedding day, or simply recalling their initial pride and pleasure of wearing it.) Either of these compliments is in tune with allowing yourself to create a positive, fulfilling here-and-now moment between you and another person.

Similarly, the next time you are at a gathering, remember that someone else's child who might seem annoying to you is their pride and joy. Search for something truthful about that child to share. Making a quick compliment on how they take good care of their favorite stuffed animal or how they managed a "please" or "thank you" will be a welcome comment to both the parent and child. And who knows, maybe this will be the compliment the child remembers and grows into, as you never know the powerful effect your words might have.

Take a little risk.

Look for opportunities to compliment others outside of your regular relationships. Begin to practice, perhaps, in safer unknown situations, such as at a large party hosted by someone you know or a business function with other colleagues in attendance. And don't feel that you have to commit to developing longer-term relationships when you strike up complimentary conversations—just plan to have a brief, pleasant encounter that raises both of your energy levels and move on. Remember: part of the reason you are complimenting others goes beyond making a kind gesture to them; the compliment is intended to boost your attitude, too, which can give you a charm-boost to make your attendance there even more successful and enjoyable.

Focus on your own joy in giving.

Again, you may be concerned about how someone you don't know will perceive your compliment. But as you tap into the emotional connectedness of all humans, the joy of complimenting will overcome this worry. Simply give. You'll get more comfortable as you go along. As attributed to Mae West, "You can do what you want, but saving love doesn't bring any interest." And as you become more secure, you'll no longer worry about how the other person might react. This is truly generous and loving.

Compliment or Come-On

Whether we like it or not, when it comes to complimenting a stranger of the opposite sex, you do need to be a bit circumspect—a little careful with a handful of judgment thrown in. The most important part is to be "on the up and up," which basically means being respectable. Ask yourself whether you expect something back for the compliment, especially if attraction is involved. For instance, you may think the local person behind the bakery counter is good looking. Should you tell them so? If you really just want to let them know how radiant their brown eyes are, go ahead. Be sure to say it with a friendly demeanor, not a stalker stare. But don't expect more than the customary customer service. Remember, a compliment interaction is not meant to be a relationship itself. And don't compliment every time you see them or it will come across as intrusive and your kind gesture will backfire.

If you truly want to get to know someone you don't know but see regularly, like a co-worker in another department, giving a few, occasional, authentic compliments signals that you see them and are paying attention. After all, science has shown that human brains are wired to prefer those who seem to be interested in us. At this point, more typical "dating rules" apply, and you may have to wait and see if they show any signs of reciprocating the interest.

In most social situations, a cheerful compliment is a pleasant, non-threatening way to break the ice with that interesting-looking person across the room. This falls into the flirting category, of course, and my best suggestion is still to be genuine and appropriate to the situation. And getting a compliment from someone else doesn't mean you owe them anything more than a quick, courteous "Thanks," if you're not interested in any further attention.

Exercise: Pick a Theme:

Try selecting a specific quality to focus on in those around you and let that guide your increased compliments. Keep the theme for a day, a week, or even a month at a time. For example, after I first complimented the bank teller on her smile after facing a long line of impatient customers, I took notice of smiles on many other people's faces. When appropriate, I would comment on them. I would say, for instance, how refreshing it was to see a smile so early in the morning (coffee shop clerk). Or what a natural smile the person had, even at the end of the day (school staff). No one knows that you might have shared a similar compliment with someone else. And you raise your compliment quotient as you go. Find other themes to compliment around by alerting your mind's reticular activator to them—a certain color people are wearing, certain phrases they say, those of certain ages or certain items others have or use, such as people wearing red, using kind words, elderly or folks' cars.

THE COMPLIMENT QUOTIENT WAY OF LIFE

CHAPTER 12

How to Take a Compliment: Five Tips for Accepting Praise

Your task is not to seek love, but merely to seek and find all the barriers within yourself that you have built against it.

~Rumi

No discussion of compliments would be complete without considering how to receive a compliment—one of the more prevalent aspects of compliments discussed these days. Just the wording we have for it—"take" a compliment—conveys that we are more than receiving; we are taking something as in a punch or a strike.

Think about the last time someone complimented you. Did you quickly try to counter their bounteous gift with a denial, a refusal, an explanation or a hesitation?

Why are many people so poor at receiving a compliment? Are we being modest when we contradict what someone says in a compliment or explain it away? Do we believe that accepting a compliment shows we are conceited or arrogant? Many thinkers and writers suggest that we are trained to hide our light out of a desire to not overshadow those around us or out of fear of what we have to live up to if everyone thinks we're brilliant. It might also have to do with the ease or preference we find in joining the common unrest or misery going on around us.

But one of the most beautiful and moving parts of compliments is the way they create a positive sensation in both the giver and recipient—and a negative reaction by the recipient dulls that sentiment for both parties. The giver may then feel compelled to heap on additional compliments (as in, "The compliment didn't take, hit the paddles again!"). Or, she may wonder if she missed the mark and should have kept her opinion to herself, further adding to the downward spiral of feeling.

An elderly neighbor, Patricia, and I are cordial and help each other out with pet sitting these days. Recently, I noticed that, after having lost her husband the year before, she had gotten a new hairdo. I happily pointed out that it was a youthful style on her and told her how attractive she looked. She smiled at the compliment but then lamented the fact that her wrinkles still gave away her age, even with the new color and cut. I immediately sensed that perhaps she had worried to herself that it was "too much" (too young? too flashy a color and style?) and she was wary of others' comments.

So while my compliment validated her hope that she had made a positive move with the change in appearance, she felt an urge to explain her worries. But I hadn't "seen" her wrinkles until she pointed them out. She's so active I had always thought of her as a wonderful role model of healthy aging and didn't focus on her laugh lines. Her questioning comment led me to add that she acted young no matter how she felt about the lines on her face and to try to buoy her up more— which is probably how most of us react when someone tries to refute our compliment to them.

Do you find yourself immediately saying, "It was nothing," after a compliment on an actual, hard-fought achievement? Or explaining away what you are wearing when someone compliments your outfit? Like others, I used to feel I had to give loads of details, in some sort of effort to prove I had earned their praise: information about how I don't usually wear these styles or how it was actually old anyway. Or I would downplay the amount of time I put into my successful work project or suggest that anyone could have done it. Maybe anyone could have done it—but not the way I did. And that was worth validating.

When I made the concerted effort to simply say "thank you," I noticed that I enjoyed the uplift of the compliment longer, and the positive atmosphere reverberated around us both. If I really felt compelled to say something back, I would say, "That is so nice of you to notice!" or "I appreciate you saying so, so much!" This way, I could keep the upward spiral of energy spinning back to the person offering the compliment.

True humility is an acceptance of your gifts and talents because you are unique. Modesty does not have to imply meekness. You can happily receive a testament to your abilities, whether creatively planning children's birthday parties or solving a quality control crisis at the office, and graciously accept the delight of a compliment. One of my daughter's expressions "du jour" (you know, a teen's go-to saying repeated more than frequently for a few months before they pick up another favorite phrase) highlights how fun and uplifting a positive response to a compliment can be for both parties. Whenever anyone comments encouragingly on something she has done, made, or bought, for instance, she quickly, and seemingly without thinking about it, smiles broadly, nods in agreement and says, "I know, right?!" Her upbeat response never sounds self-serving or egotistical (a concern we grown-ups tend to have when agreeing with someone commending us on our good taste or good work). She simply revels in the obvious good-fortune of the item or action when acknowledged, making the compliment fun for all.

When thinking about how to receive a compliment, take heed of how *you* feel when you *give* a compliment. You want the recipient to enjoy it, not negate it, right? And also, remember that when you step into your genius, you give others permission to be fully themselves, too. *Smart thinking,* you say? *I know, right?!*

Complimentology Tips

FIVE TIPS FOR ACCEPTING PRAISE

Stop offering extraneous information.

When you are given a compliment, find a way to "bite your tongue." Remind yourself not to offer any explanations, caveats or hesitations. Of course, you will probably want to reply with a statement of thanks or acknowledgment of some kind, such as, "I appreciate you noticing," or simply, "Thank you!" Or, you may take the window of opportunity to give a compliment back to them, but only with a genuine, authentic comment.

Shorten self-deprecating responses.

If you are tempted to try to balance your gratitude with humility by being self deprecating, be careful. If you go on and on about not deserving the commendation, your self-deprecating behavior ends up trivializing what they said to you or comes across as false humility and you've just canceled out the warm glow for both of you. Stick to the gracious, "Thank you."

Focus on the gift you will give back.

If you are having a hard time simply accepting a compliment, try to remember that the person complimenting you is getting a highly vibrational burst of energy from the generosity of their comment, which is magnified by your cordial acceptance. Allow them the opportunity to enjoy the moment. "Return gift" the energy of their compliment by accepting it at the least courteously and hopefully, happily.

Channel Self-Confidence

An appreciative acknowledgment of a compliment conveys healthy self-esteem rather than seeming self-centered. Remember that self-confidence is attractive to others, and nothing communicates your sense of self as appropriately as accepting praise graciously. You might refute or negate praise out of humility yet others might interpret it as insecurity. Don't take the compliment, and then go on and on about how great you are, of course. But responding to a compliment simply and graciously is construed positively by others.

Tie into the mirror effect.

By graciously accepting someone's compliment, you are in essence being a mirror, reminding that person that we all have worthwhile gifts. Think about how your acceptance is contributing to the rising tide that lifts all of our boats of brilliance.

CHAPTER THIRTEEN

Creating a Compliment Culture

Person to person, moment to moment,
as we love, we change the world.

~Samahria Lyte Kaufman

When something comes to life in others
because of you, then you have made
an approach to immortality.

~Norman Cousins

ountless self-help books and other spiritual, personal development, career or psychology texts are written every year about finding our purpose. After reading that sentence, you may have already flashed to at least one title that you have on your bookshelf or heard about from a friend. They are based on the premise that each of us is here to bring our own, unique gifts to the world. How exciting! I've come to cherish the idea that, by honoring our uniqueness, we learn the perfect way to live authentically and find fulfillment. And in our living out our individual purposes in unique ways, we all bring a capacity to heal the world. I'll repeat it, *to heal the world*. If that sounds too lofty or leaves you skeptical, how about accepting that you're at least here to heal *your corner* of the world?

Why are compliments part of this healing? Because by tapping into the heart-centered power of a compliment connection and letting the grit of the relationship sift away, we enable ourselves to touch the highest and best in others. This is love talking. This is a compliment at its finest.

Certified Coach and Energy Leadership™ Master Practitioner Darla LeDoux walked me through the seven levels of energy leadership to understand a bit more about how the power of compliments actually raises us up into higher energy states, where we reach our capacity to live more authentically and non-judgmentally. As it turns out, many of us stay in lower levels where, whether we realize it or not, we blame others, fear others, criticize others, and attack others.

"A compliment can move you up three to five levels immediately," Darla says. It frees us from the negativity of the lower levels and increases our probability of responding to life at that higher-level energy into the future. "So every time you freely give a compliment, you are choosing a new future for yourself," she adds.

So how does *this* future sound: You achieve more effective communication. You reduce misunderstandings that may lead to further problems. You bolster your relationships with all of your loved ones and colleagues. You attain a sense of emotional freedom and safety. And you grow the love around you.

What future do you want to create? Choosing to grace your interactions with simple, positive words is one easy, but substantial, means of joining the ranks of healers among us.

The compliment is an elegant, essential part of your goal to:

Uplift—even for a moment

Soothe—by bridging the gulf between you and others

Enliven—by amping up the quality of
your interactions

Give—by taking yourself out of your daily concerns and focusing on others.

You never know how or when your compliment will affect someone. By speaking up, you may be changing the very current in someone's life.

Recently I decided to take the opportunity to refinance my home. Because it was something out of my knowledge base and comfort zone, I was leery about the whole undertaking. After making queries about the web-based options, my bank's services, and so on, I received a quick, professional response from a local mortgage broker. Having an affinity for small-business people, I took a second to look at his materials. They weren't glossy but appeared professional, with facts, testimonials and credentials. Later, after we met in person, I knew right away that Shawn was the person I would trust to help me navigate today's muddy waters of the mortgage world.

Because he seemed so genuinely concerned with covering all of the issues, I became more comfortable asking what I thought were those dumb questions—questions to which surely someone my age who already owned a home would know the answers. As we talked more, his passion for the details, his concern about helping each client, his nonjudgmental demeanor and his clear mission to do the best job possible greatly impressed me. While we were wrapping up, I had to quickly assess whether or not to pass along a compliment on Shawn's knowledge and abilities. The cons ran through my head: Would he think I was flirting with him? Was it really necessary or appropriate to compliment someone I was paying to help me?

I'm sure by now you've guessed that I went ahead with my praise: I took a deep breath and jumped in, giving him a compliment—well, actually three. I praised him for how he clearly knew what he was talking about, how he was very easy to talk to, and how I thought people would react positively to his message and personal style. Had he ever thought about putting on seminars or other speaking events?

A sheepish grin crossed his face, and Shawn proceeded to tell me how he had been thinking of talking to people in larger groups. As a matter of fact, he had already been checking into training. He was clearly gratified that I had shared my impression of him and his work.

The next time we met to sign the pile of paperwork, he told me that he had started his speaker's coaching. He noted that he was pleased that I had said something as it helped push him into taking action. Once again, mighty heavy lifting on the part of a little extra time, focus and praise.

Can you think of examples of memorable compliments that impacted your own life? The first flattering remark from your husband. An unexpectedly timed compliment from your child. Praise from a boss or important client in front of your colleagues. An unusually perceptive remark from a friend.

When you look back on your life, you will find that the moments you felt most alive and engaged with your life's purpose are those moments when you gave or accepted something in the spirit of love. Leo Buscaglia, author and love guru, stated, "For a moment, love can change the world."

In this stressed out, demanding world, finding quality time, or sometimes virtually any time, with loved ones is difficult. But nearly everyone can find an extra minute to convey a positive, uplifting compliment. Not only does the receiver feel your love and support, but you strengthen your bonds with your family, friends and community.

Do you feel the call to live your positive purpose for yourself and for those around you? Are you concerned with contributing to a more respectful, tolerant vibration in the world? Do you desire more happiness and personal fulfillment?

When you build this simple but powerful compliment practice, when you adopt this heart-centered, positive, focused way of connecting to others, you don't just set an upward spiral in motion, you also attract more abundance and positive people into your life! Whether you join the ranks of us all-out complimenters or simply become more in tune with the power of praise, you will easily reap the benefits of the routine practice of giving more praise and compliments to others, a practice that can bring you a life of greater harmony and success.

As with any change, regular action is required to build this into a habitual way of approaching the world. There will be gremlins along the way, waiting to trip you up into negativity, complaints or criticism. At these times, go back to the basics and reinvigorate your compliment habit. Take a few minutes to remember its simple, powerful parameters.

Like the "get out of jail free" Monopoly card you're happy to draw because you never know when a roll of the dice will put you behind the corner-square bars, you have the ability to offer up a compliment on a difficult day and boost your spirits or even change the atmosphere around you. In other words, you can compliment your way into the love and kindness you want to reap while generously sharing that love and kindness with others.

Decide to raise your compliment quotient. Aim to uplift your part of the planet. Commit to upgrading your language and your interactions. Dare to live your dreams, your values, your intention to have a closely-knit family, a more romantically connected marriage or love relationship, and a more loving interaction with the world. Watch out—raising your compliment quotient is habit forming!

You are brilliant.

BIBLIOGRAPHY

Ban Breathnach, Sarah. *Simple Abundance A Daybook of Comfort and Joy.*
New York: Warner Books Inc., 1995

Britten, Rhonda. *Fearless Living ™ Live Without Excuses and Love Without Regret.*
New York: Dutton, Penguin Putnam Inc, 2001

Edlund, Dr. Matthew. *The Power of Rest Why Sleep Alone is Not Enough.*
New York: HarperOne, 2010

Godeck, Greg. *1001 Ways to be Romantic.*
Naperville, Illinois: Sourcebook Inc., 1999

Jeffers, Susan. *Feel the Fear and Do It Anyway™.*
New York: Ballantine Books, 2006

Mandino, Og. *The Greatest Salesman in the World.*
New York: Bantam Books, Inc., 1974

Maslow, Abraham. *Motivation and Personality.*
New York: Harper, 1954

Masterson, Michael. *Ready, Fire, Aim Zero to $100 Million in No Time Flat.*
Hoboken, New Jersey: John Wiley & Sons, 2008

Nightingale, Earl. *Lead the Field.*
New York: bnpublishing, 2007

O'Donohue, John. *Anam Cara-A Book of Celtic Wisdom.*
New York City: HarperCollins, 1998

Pay it Forward. Movie.
Warner Brothers Pictures and Bel Air Entertainment, 2000. Based on the book by Catherine Ryan Hyde. New York: Simon & Schuster, 1999

Richardson, Cheryl. *Life Makeovers*.
    New York: Broadway Books, 2000

Roxanne. Movie.
    Columbia Pictures, 1987

"Soul Series." *The OprahWinfrey Show*. Oprah Winfrey.
    Harpo Productions Inc. 17 Feb. 2010

Vitale, Dr. Joe. *Attract Money Now*.
    Austin, Texas: Hypnotic Marketing, Inc. 2010

Williamson, Marianne. *A Return to Love*.
    New York: HarperCollins Publishers, Inc., 1992

Zadra, Dan. *Be The Difference*.
    Seattle, Washington: Compendium, Inc. 2006

Quotations not attributed were gathered over the years from emails, shared from friends or gathered on quotation websites, such as ThinkExist.com and quote-garden.com. My sincere thanks to authors, contributors and other sources, and where appropriate, my apologies for incorrect attributions.

GRATITUDES

*Kindness is the golden chain by which
society is bound together.*

~Goethe

Extending my deepest thanks to the following people for helping The Compliment Quotient book become a reality.

Nancy Cleary, Wyatt-MacKenzie Publishing, Inc., the savvy publishing guru and business woman for generously sharing her expertise and advice, turning a writer into an author along the way

Lisa Tener, book writing coach and muse par none, who believed first so whole heartedly in *The Compliment Quotient* and taught a fledgling author to bring the vision of her book to life.

Darla LeDoux, a brilliant life coach, on whom I have relied for insightful guidance, support and friendship along the pathway of finding my sweet spot and bringing my gifts to the world.

Tama Kieves, for sharing enlightened, spirit-filled guidance in person and with beautiful words, helping me to put my heart-felt desire into the river.

Patti Thorn, editor and wordsmith, who was relentless and generous in helping me convey my truth in my most positive, professional voice and became a friend along the way.

Kelly Johnson, for her gracious, friendly business assistance extraordinaire.

Meghan Simpson, for her most amazing graphic and web design talents and friendship.

Heather Allard, for long-distance encouragement and connection along my mom-preneur pathway.

Sonya Derian, for stimulating me to live out loud and bring my message to the world.

Gerry Wolfson-Grande, an expert copy editor for quick and precise proofreading.

Teresa Skaggs with DesignZone USA for creative, beautiful layout and design.

Allison Billings, Gina Fenske, Kristi Johnson and Susie Russell, and the "cookie bake" crew for being great women and sharing friendship along the way.

Deep abiding love and gratitude to my friends Happy Harrington, Joy Fitzgerald and Pat Pugh for being my soul-sister companions through life and loving me through all my rough-draft stages, book and all.

My siblings Kimberly Baker, Melanie and Greg Widmar, Andrea Hird, Jill Rojek, and Tony and Angie Rojek for always being there as proof of love and generous support and friendship.

My children Tori, Blake and Kelsie for their continual patience throughout the late nights, early mornings and distracted days finishing "just a little more writing." You have taught me about patience, bliss and unconditional love, always.

My parents, Leo and Lorraine Rojek, for their neverending love and practical guidance through all the "knowledge bumps" along the way.

My Celtic companion, John Kilbane, who inspires me with his heart and humor, and with whom I share love unendingly, not anyway, but because.

For everyone who has ever given me a compliment or inspired a compliment from me along the way, for their encouragement and kindness.

ABOUT THE AUTHOR

Monica Strobel

...draws on a wealth of professional expertise, practicality and passions in her book, *The Compliment Quotient*, and all of her creative endeavors. She is dedicated to empowering busy women to get more joy into and out of their lives and relationships.

Monica has long been recognized for her positive, can-do attitude and habit of saying nice things. She has always focused on leaving the world a better place, throughout a 25-year career in environmental, older adults and children's issues.

She is a passionate mom-preneur, seasoned writer and charismatic speaker. People find themselves telling her all kinds of things as she makes others feel at home and appreciated!

She is the founder of *Generations In Touch* and *Sammy the Mail Snail Club*, designed to enhance connections between kids and grandparents and ease the stress on busy parents, www.generationsintouch.com.

Monica grew up in the Chicago metro area, graduated from University of Colorado at Boulder, and resides in the Denver area, loving the Rocky Mountain lifestyle and inspiring her three children to put their best foot forward, find something positive to say and always know which way is west.

```
┌─────────────────────────────────┐
│        More Success             │
│         with the                │
│    Compliment Coach             │
└─────────────────────────────────┘
```

Move ahead in your life and relationships with more Compliment Quotient resources:

The Busy Woman's Six-Week Guide to More Romance, More Connection, More Joy

Claim a more joyful life, be the loving presence you want to be, flourish in all your relationships! This home study course is designed to give you specific, practical tools and exercises to make an immediate difference in your life and reap more enjoyment along the way. Simply open a weekly email for six weeks, do the short lesson with video and exercises through the week. Six weeks to more loving, more lightness and more impact.

Uplevel Your Language for Success 7-Hour eCourse

This one-week e-class is a quick but comprehensive guide to immediately transform your compliment style and ability to garner success in your relationships, your career and social interactions. One email lesson and one half-hour per day, for one week, to better language your loving and brilliant self.

Visit www.complimentquotient.com/resources for information to get started today!

Free Resources

Receive my FREE email newsletter filled with compliment tips and articles. Get a *Free Compliments* flyer, to have some fun spreading compliments at home or the office. www.complimentquotient.com.

Share Your Compliments success

Nothing makes me happier than hearing about you and your compliments: the best one you've ever gotten, who you compliment the most or another nugget of compliment success you've had after reading this book.

Please visit www.complimentquotient.com and send your comments via the Contact Form or email me at monica@complimentquotient.com with your stories or questions.

Or write to *The Compliment Quotient*, WiseRoads Press, PO Box 3615, Littleton, CO 80122

Speaking

Conferences, college, corporate and wellness.

Monica Strobel, The Compliment Coach, is available for interactive public or corporate presentations and speaking engagements, for civic or trade association meetings, corporate wellness programs, meeting and convention spouses programming, more.

Please contact Monica at:

monica@complimentquotient.com

The Compliment Quotient is available in bulk or as customized orders for company premiums, promotional items, gifts, employee incentives, educational tools and charitable contributions. Please contact the author for more information. monica@complimentquotient.com

Order more copies of *The Compliment Quotient*: *Boost Your Spirits, Spark Your Relationships and Uplift the World*, for your family, friends, co-workers, club or giveaway.

✂ ORDER FORM

Name _____

Email _____

SHIPPING ADDRESS:

City _____

State _____ Zip _____

BILLING ADDRESS: (if different)

City _____

State _____ Zip _____

Number of books _____ x $14.95 = _____

plus shipping _____ = $ _____ **TOTAL DUE**

SHIPPING:

1-3 books $2.95 · 2-6 books $ 4.95 · 7-10 books $8.95 · 11 + please call

Payment Method: ❏ Check   ❏ Visa   ❏ MC

CC# _____

Exp. Date _____ Ver. Code _____

Name on Card _____

Signature _____

MAIL TO: *The Compliment Quotient*, **WiseRoads Press, PO Box 3615, Littleton, CO 80122**

You will receive an email confirmation when shipped. Please allow up to two weeks for delivery.

Your information is held in secure confidence – never shared with anyone else.

CPSIA information can be obtained at www.ICGtesting.com
Printed in the USA
BVOW061341020412

286602BV00001B/2/P